Schnellboot

Written by David L. Krakow

In Action®

Cover Art by Don Greer
Perspective Illustrations by Alin
Line Illustrations by David L. Krakow

Squadron Signal®
Publications

(Front Cover) Camouflaged for daylight operations and making high speed in search of Soviet shipping in the Baltic, this early unarmored S 38 represents the most common type of Schnellboot deployed by the Kriegsmarine.

(Back Cover) An S 100 class Schnellboot attacks British merchant ships in the English Channel in 1944. This was the lead boat in the last major Schnellboote class deployed during World War II. The 4th S-Bootsflottille's panther insignia is painted on the midship's bulkhead.

About the In Action® Series

In Action® books, despite the title of the genre, are books that trace the development of a single type of aircraft, armored vehicle, or ship from prototype to the final production variant. Experimental or "one-off" variants can also be included. Our first *In Action*® book was printed in 1971.

 Hardcover ISBN 978-0-89747-661-4
Softcover ISBN 978-0-89747-660-7
Proudly printed in the U.S.A.
Copyright 2013 Squadron/Signal Publications
1115 Crowley Drive, Carrollton, TX 75006-1312 U.S.A.

Military/Combat Photographs and Snapshots

If you have any photos of aircraft, armor, soldiers, or ships of any nation, particularly wartime snapshots, why not share them with us and help make Squadron/Signal's books all the more interesting and complete in the future? Any photograph sent to us will be copied and returned. Electronic images are preferred. The donor will be fully credited for any photos used. Please send them to:

Squadron/Signal Publications
1115 Crowley Drive
Carrollton, TX 75006-1312 U.S.A.
www.SquadronSignalPublications.com

(Title Page) An armored S 38 class S-Boot makes a fast run to base at daybreak. Schnellboote usually operated at night where there was less of a threat from aircraft and surface ships. It carries a 2cm cannon on the foredeck, a 7.92mm MG34 Zwillingslafette (twin mount) amidships, and a shielded 2cm weapon aft. The censor has removed this boat's flotilla number '6.' (PK Rolf Kröncke via PT Boats, Inc. collection)

Acknowledgments

We gratefully acknowledge the assistance of: Lise Alring, Erik-Jan Bakker, Brian Balkwill, R.W. Brown, the late Admiral Hermann Büchting, T. Garth Connelly, Dr. Peter De Laet, Ola Erlandsson, Ernest Graystone, Alyce Mary Guthrie, Donald Heller, Günter Huff, John Klein, Maksim Kosover, Erich Krogh, Maurice Laarman, John Lambert, Robert Lockie, Francis MacNaughton, Bruce Marshall, Richard Mundt, Dr. Christian Ostersehlte, Dr. Steve Rohan, Dr. Al Ross II, Alin S., Pia Sørensen, Peter Tamm, Kevin Wheatcroft, John Wheeler, Frank Wiemers, Danish Naval Base Korsoer, Danish Naval Library, Lürssen GmbH, The Naval War College, PT Boats, Inc., Royal Danish Navy, U.S. Army Ordnance Museum, and U.S. Navy Historical Center. All unattributed photographs come from the D. Krakow collection.

Introduction

Developments in the internal combustion engine, the invention of the torpedo, the restrictions of the Versailles treaty, British naval hegemony, and an American contract for a luxury yacht are but some of the forces of history that shaped what is generally considered the best motor torpedo boat (MTB) of World War II. Sometimes referred to as the "S-Boat" or by the archaic Royal Navy term "E-Boat," the Schnellboot was a formidable assembly of technology, naval architecture, and highly-trained men.

Almost immediately after the First World War ended, German military strategists set about planning for the next war. Although the Treaty of Versailles was meant to prevent Germany from taking up arms in a war of aggression, its practical effect was to stimulate an ingenious and advanced arms development program. Working in secret, German engineers designed weapons that both circumvented the restrictions of the Versailles treaty and capitalized on technologies and tactics that could enable a small, well-equipped nation to defeat rapidly a more powerful but outdated enemy.

An extensive clandestine naval research and development program was initiated by Admiral Paul Behnke, commander-in-chief of the Reichsmarine (the Weimar Republic's Navy), using black funds garnered from the sale of scrapped warships. In order to maintain secrecy, Behnke authorized a confidant, Kapitän zur See Walter Lohmann, to operate entirely on his own initiative, warning him the Navy would allege Lohmann had acted without orders, should his activities be exposed.

Meanwhile, the German naval command, considering the severe limitations of the peace treaty and capitalizing on its limited experience with light motor gun boats (MGBs) and MTBs at Zeebrugge, called for the development of a boat suited for combat in North Sea conditions. The Versailles treaty did not specifically address MTBs (the great powers evidently considered such small boats unimportant) nevertheless, the project was kept secret behind bogus civilian yacht clubs and corporations created and funded by Lohmann. Despite specific proposals for the next generation of MTB made by naval engineers at the end of the First World War, in 1923 the Navy called for a broad spectrum of designs.

Most initial proposals concentrated on the short planing hulls commonly used for speedboats. This surface skimming design is ideal for fast boats in calm waters but loses its

Terminology

The German term Schnellboot (literally "speedboat") and its German abbreviation S-Boot are used throughout, along with the plural Schnellboote and S-Boote, in preference to the hybrid German/English terms "S-boat" and S-boats. Specifications and dimensions are metric. Speeds are, by convention, in knots (1 nautical mile per hour, equivalent to 1.85km/h) and displacements are given as tons standard displacement. Many of the photographs included here were taken by German military photographers who belonged to a Propaganda Kompanie (PK). They are credited on the photos as PK+the photographer's surname.

chief advantage of efficiency when waves slam against the flat hull bottom. Furthermore, weight is a critical issue, and the iridescent plume of water created by a planing boat moving at high speed is visible over great distances at night, a feature clearly undesirable for a stealthy military vessel.

One such boat, designated "Experimental Boat K" was built by Abeking & Rasmussen along the lines of the Royal Navy's 55ft Thornycroft Coastal Motor Boat in 1926. It was approximately 18.3 metres long and displaced 16 tons. Two 450 h.p. gasoline engines powered two shafts, giving the boat a maximum speed of close to 40 knots. The main armament was a pair of 45.7cm torpedoes firing aft, thus following the British design. A proposal for forward-firing torpedoes envisioned a pair of roll-off side launching rails after the Italian method. The double-planked mahogany construction was typical for torpedo boats of that period but not substantial enough to prevent damage and leaking, even at 25 knots in calm seas. Attempts to strengthen the hull were unsuccessful. This boat and several others tested by the Navy further underscored the superiority of the round-bilged displacement hull over the hard chine V-bottom design used by most other nations.

Concurrent with Experimental Boat K, the well known yacht-building firm of Lürssen built a boat at its own expense in 1925/26. Named Lür, this boat was approximately 19.8 metres long, had a beam of approximately 2.7 metres and a draft of 0.9 meters. She displaced 23 tons and with three 450 h.p. Maybach engines achieved a top speed of 33.5 knots. The hull was built of mahogany and had a round bilged design that was similar to the "Express Motor Cruiser" that had been successfully marketed to wealthy Americans

A Kaiserliche Marine (Imperial German Navy) Motor Gun Boat (MGB) is moored at Zeebrugge, Belgium, in 1917. The vessel is armed with a bow-mounted 7.92mm MG08/15 machine gun. Zeebrugge – located in the Belgian region of Flanders – was a base of German naval operations in the North Sea. This and other light vessels saw little action during World War I. Their limited experience was, however, factored into the Schnellboot concept after the conflict. (A. Stegitz)

in the 1920s. The rounded bilge displacement hull design proved to be well suited for operations in the North Sea and Baltic waters.

In 1928, in light of these experiments and the dismal North Sea weather, the German naval command elected to concentrate strictly on a round-bottomed displacement hull. Its attention was drawn to a highly innovative motor yacht built by the German boatyard Lürssen for the German-American banking tycoon Otto Herman Kahn. Its round-bottomed hull was 22.5m long and displaced 22.5 tons. It reached a top speed of 34 knots, making it the world's fastest boat in its class at the time. It was named Oheka II after the owner's monogram and in it, Lürrsen overcame many of the drawbacks of the round-bottomed displacement hull. The boat ploughed through the water by the brute force of three 550 h.p. Maybach engines and the composite construction of wood planks over alloy frames reduced weight. The inefficient tendency for round hulls to 'squat' stern-down at high speeds was counterbalanced by an underwater hull form that flattened towards the stern, providing hydrodynamic lift where it was needed.

Oheka II's combination of speed, strength and seaworthiness was precisely what the naval command wanted. In addition, the large displacement would minimize the balance effects of carrying and firing two heavy torpedoes far forward of the hull's center of gravity. In November 1929, Lürssen was given a contract to build a boat to the same basic design but with two detachable torpedo tubes on the forecastle, a slightly improved top speed and other minor differences. It commissioned as the UZ (S) 16, later renamed S 1. The S 1 was the Kriegsmarine's first true MTB and the basis for all other S-Boote built during World War II.

Oheka II (1927)

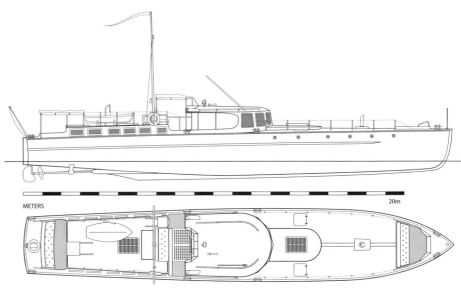

The aggressive spirit of the Schnellboot fleet is typified in this prewar view of S 19. This S 18 class vessel has black hull numbers, which were overpainted for security reasons after World War II began. Experiments dating back to the mid-1920s led to the Schnellboot – a highly capable motor torpedo boat optimized for both North Sea and Baltic Sea conditions.

Development and Comparison

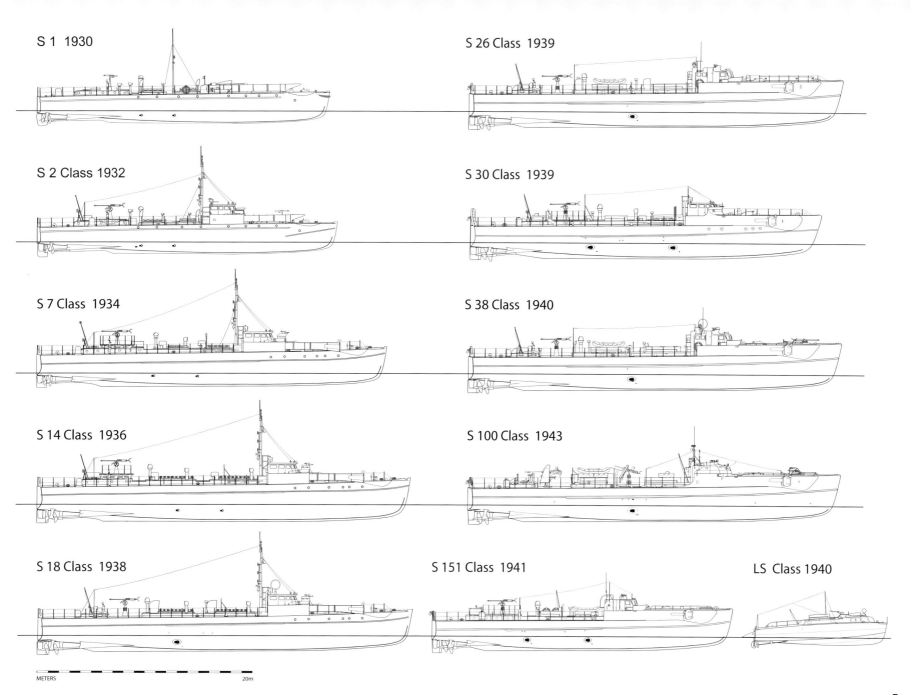

S 1 1930

S 2 Class 1932

S 7 Class 1934

S 14 Class 1936

S 18 Class 1938

S 26 Class 1939

S 30 Class 1939

S 38 Class 1940

S 100 Class 1943

S 151 Class 1941

LS Class 1940

METERS   20m

UZ (S)16 is in its original, open-bridge configuration upon commissioning at the Lürssen boatyard in August, 1930. For political reasons, it was designated a "Sub Chaser" and the torpedo tubes were not fixed in place. In March 1932, as Germany pushed back against Allied restrictions, secrecy was dropped and the boat was renamed S 1. The prototype for all Schnellboote, its relatively large size gave S 1 superior sea-keeping and endurance.

S 4 flies the 1933 pattern Reichsmarine naval ensign – a black, white, and red tricolor with a black Iron Cross. The flag was replaced on 9 November 1935. The S 2 class boat S 4 displayed several improvements over the S 1, including the addition of front shutters to the torpedo tubes. (A. Klein)

S 1

S 1 commissioned on 7 August 1930 and was referred to by the simple cover name "Schnellboot" which eventually became the official classification for this type of vessel. It was was a round-bilged design built of mahogany and light metal composite, capable of high speed, even in heavy seas. Power was provided by three Daimler-Benz BFz V-12 cylinder four-stroke gasoline engines each of 800 h.p. - 900 h.p., and a 100-h.p. Maybach auxiliary engine for quiet running. S 1 had a 12-man crew. At 39.8 tons; it was the largest high-speed coastal motor boat of its day. It was originally designed with an open steering platform, and removable torpedo rubes. After extensive testing, refits included fixed tubes and an enclosed wheelhouse.

S 1 proved an excellent and versatile design with a superior range of 582 nautical miles at 22 knots and sea keeping at up to Beaufort Sea State 5. Experimentation with S 1 and the initial batch of five boats led to immediate improvements and innovations. S 1 was sold to Spain in 1938.

S 2 class (S 2 through S 5)

S 2 to S 5 were delivered to the German navy between April and July 1932. While similar to the S 1, they were slightly longer and had a 46.5-ton displacement to facilitate an improved layout and additional equipment. Another improvement was the addition of superchargers to the BFz V-12 powerplant. The superchargers increased engine output to 1,100 h.p.

A key innovation introduced with S 2 was the addition of a special rudder arrangement. To port and starboard of the main rudder were two smaller rudders that could be angled outboard by up to 30°. At high speed, the angled rudders drew a ventilation air pocket slightly behind the three propellers, increasing their efficiency, reducing stern wake, and keeping the boat's pitch closer to horizontal, a phenomenon which became known as the Lürssen Effekt.

The four boats designated S 2 to S 5 formed the nucleus of the First Schnellboot Sub-Flotilla and were immediately put to use for intensive training and tactics development. Each boat had a 12-man crew. When more modern types became available in 1938, S 2 to S 5 were sold to Spain. An additional three boats based on this type were constructed for export to China, five for Bulgaria, and eight for Yugoslavia. These vessels were modified to include such features as a bow knuckle.

S 6

S 6 was an enlarged, 60.4-ton version of the previous class designed around the first available diesel engine, the MAN L7. While S 6 served adequately as an engine testbed, it was not a particularly successful design and this vessel was also sold to Spain in 1938. Deficiencies noted in S 6 and earlier boats contributed to significant improvements in the next classes.

Three stages of Schnellboot evolution are well-illustrated in this mid-1935 view looking down from Flotilla Tender *Tsingtau* anchored off Travemünde. S 3 (top) which commissioned in May 1932, displays the smaller proportions and sharp bow of an early vessel. S 8 (middle) is a first type S 7 class boat which commissioned in September 1934. This type, which weighed almost 30 tons more than S 3, is identified by the three cylindrical engine room ventilators arranged over its MAN L7 motors. S 10 (bottom) is a second type S 7 class boat which commissioned in March 1935. This type was powered by superior MB 502 engines and had three distinctive, oblong-shaped ventilators centered above the engine rooms. While S 3 has new torpedo tubes, and all three have new RZA 3 torpedo sights, signal platforms have not yet been fitted on the wheelhouses.

The S 7 class vessels S 9, S 10, and S 11 display their improved bow design while berthed in the Spring of 1937. High on the masts, V- and X-shaped insignia were used for visual boat identification within the Flotilla. Three pairs of red and white lamps below were used for night signaling. White hull numbers were painted on the bows.

The same group of Schnellboote is moored to Wilhelmshaven's Bontekai quay, aft of their flotilla tender *Tsingtau*. The Reichskriegsflagge (war ensign) flies from their stern flagstaffs, while the Gösch (naval jack) flies from the jackstaff of another S-Boot, and a number 8 (watch duty) pennant flies from S 9's yardarm.

S 7 Class (S 7 through S 13)

These 75.8-ton vessels were built along the lines of the S 6 but with the increased reserve buoyancy of a knuckle added at the bow. This modification prevented the vessel from nosing into waves in foul weather. S 7 through S 13, which entered service from October 1934 to December 1935, are divided into two subtypes. The seven-cylinder MAN L7 engines that powered the S 7, S 8, and S 9 were not powerful enough to meet the navy's requirements, so boats S 10 through S 13 received the more successful 16-cylinder MB 502 engine. Externally they differed only in engine room ventilator arrangements.

S 14 Class (S 14 through S 17)

Built from 1936 to 1938, the four 92-ton boats of the S 14 class were based on the previous class but enlarged to accommodate an 11-cylinder MAN L11 engine, a motor that proved problematic and reduced range and reliability. These boats were deployed during the war as sub chasers.

S 18 Class (S 18 through S 25)

Similar to the preceding class, the eight S 18 class boats built from 1938 to 1939 were powered by the advanced 20-cylinder Mercedes MB 501, enabling these vessels to reach a maximum speed of almost 40 knots. This class added a wedge to the lower stern to deflect water flow slightly downwards, countering the hull's tendency to settle into the water as speed increased. The addition of the wedge was the final stage in development of the S-Boot's hull lines. Individual boats of this class differed in ventilator types.

S 1 (post refit)

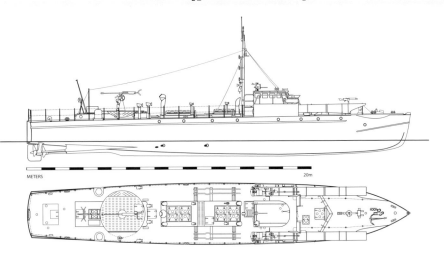

METERS   20m

S 9 and S 11 display early light-gray paint schemes as they lie alongside each other. The wooden planked decks are finished with a layer of canvas permeated with special waterproof and wear-resistant dark gray paint. Numerals are white on the lower bows. The small S 9 and S 11 on the upper bows are brass fixtures. S 9's hull is a slightly lighter gray than is its superstructure.

S 11 cuts through its leader's wake during pre-war exercises. (W. Andres)

In 1937-1938, black hull numbers replaced white numbers on S 16 and other Schnellboote, when these vessels were repainted in the new near-white color designated Schnellbootweiß. (Lürssen)

S 2 Class

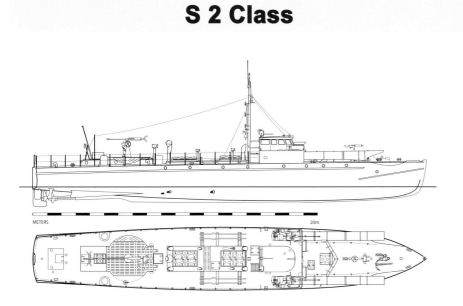

METERS   20m

This packet of three 2nd type S 7 class boats are newly prepared for war with air recognition markings and radio antennas moved to the mast top for increased range. Refits prior to 1939 have added signalman's platforms aft of the wheelhouses. This view from the flotilla tender shows many other interesting details such as the 2nd type engine room ventilator arrangement, an RZA 3 torpedo sight, early Bosch sirens on the masts, and the rigid undersides of the life rafts. Over the deckhouses are wooden walkway gratings with oval slots, typical of meticulous pre war manufacture. Later boats featured simplified plank walkways. The boats are painted Schnellbootweiß overall with light gray decks and dark gray gratings. Kriegsmarine regulations specified wooden gratings to be coated with a preservative, then painted a scuff and slip-resistant gray paint. The 2cm gun platform gratings are covered with mats to increase traction and protect the woodwork.

S 7 Class (2nd Type)

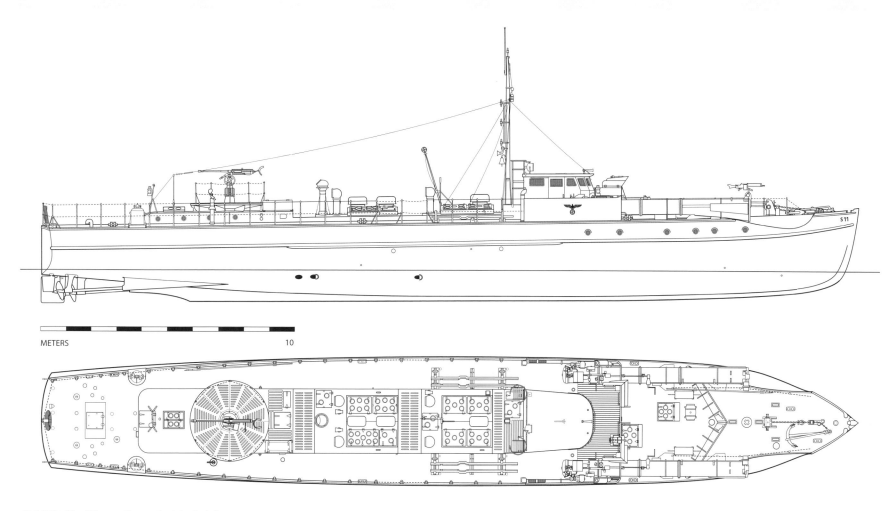

METERS   10

Mast, rigging & bow MG removed from overhead view for clarity.

Specifications

Length: .... 32. 36 meters
Beam: .... 4.9 meters
Draught: .... 1.2 meters
Displacement: ...... 75 tons, 86 tons fully loaded
Powerplant: .... 3 x Daimler Benz MB 502
Speed: .... 35 knots maximum

Range: .... 750 nautical miles
Armament: ..... 2 x 53.3cm torpedo tubes, up to 4 torpedoes.
                        1 x 2cm aft, 1 x MG 08/15 on bow pedistal.
Crew: 18

Responding to reconnaissance reports of cargo vessels attempting to hide in fjords north of Bergen, this 2nd type S 7 class S-Boot on interdiction patrol changes course off Botnane, Norway, on 13 May 1940. The S-Boote turned primarily using the rudder, although differential engine power to its three propellers could be employed for tight and emergency maneuvers. (PK Rolf Kröncke)

An S 7 class vessel makes a high-speed run off the Norwegian coast in May 1940. Hull numbers were painted over for security when the Second World War started. Although outdated by rapid design developments, the early S-Boote performed important patrol and escort duties during the conflict. (PK Rolf Kröncke)

A 2nd type S 7 class S-boot has pulled alongside the Norwegian freighter *Bera* found hiding in Norway's Sørgulen fjord, near Svelgen, on 13 May 1940. Bound for Weston Point, Britain, with 950 tons of calcium carbide, *Bera* was sent to Hamburg as a war prize. Merchant ships were helpless against the S-Boot's weapons. (PK Rolf Kröncke)

The S 14 class boat S 15 cruises off the German coast prior to World War II. Canvas dodgers on the railing protect the torpedo cradles from seawater. Cast bronze Reichsadler (national eagle insignia) are mounted to the bulwarks outboard of the wheelhouse. These emblems were removed after the outbreak of the conflict. (A. Klein)

S 14 Class

An S 14 class wheelhouse contains an engine order telegraph, tachometer, wheel and compass in the standard layout for all classes of S-Boot. Interior bulkheads are finished in semi gloss black paint and varnished mahogany. The photographer's flash has bounced off the traditional polished brass surfaces of the instruments. (Lürssen)

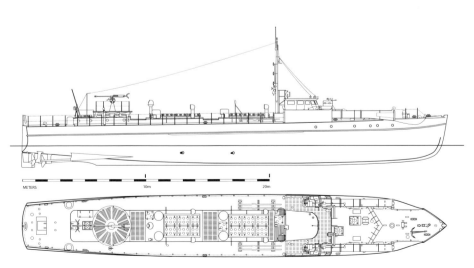

METERS   10m   20m

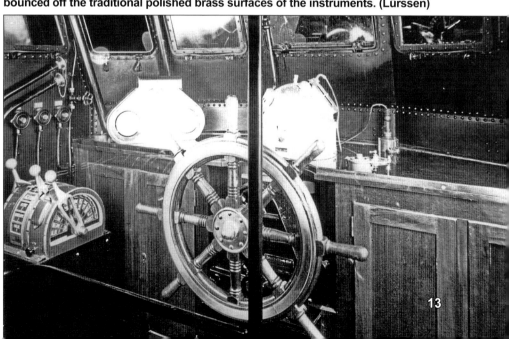

13

The S 18 class S 19 crests the wake of the leader in a pre-war exercise. Two wing rudders and a stern wedge ordinarily counteracted the tendency for these boats to nose up at speed. Wing rudders worked with the larger main rudder for lateral control of the vessel. This class introduced the stern wedge that became standard on later Schnellboote. (Ferdinand Urbahns)

S 19 makes speed on a prewar exercise. The white bow number has been removed by a censor. What appears to be a boot topping in the photo is actually oil staining at the water line.

Crewmen of S 18 pause for lunch while on a 1942 training mission to Stettin with the new 7th Flotilla. The S 18 class was the last to have sliding racks that enabled torpedoes to be stowed neatly inboard against the deckhouses. The low-profile ventilators over the engine rooms were standard on later classes. Signal flags are stowed in pockets sewn to the inboard side of the dodger at far left. The clover-leaf shaped object is a skylight blackout cover.

S 18 Class

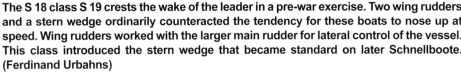

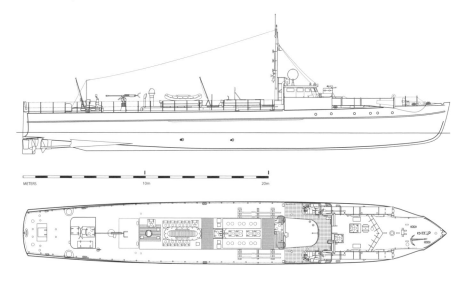

METERS   10m   20m

S 26 Class (S 26 through S 29)

Built from 1939 to 1940, the 92.5-ton S 26 class boats continued the S 18 class, but marked a leap forward in design due to significant changes in the superstructure. The torpedo tubes were enclosed in a decked-over forecastle, increasing interior space and reserve buoyancy. The extra half-meter of freeboard also kept the boats drier. A raised, open bridge set into the wheelhouse roof afforded the commander a centralized position with better visibility and more shelter than in previous designs, in which he stood forward of the wheelhouse. Two swing-out seats and a wooden grating over the deck offered some comfort. The torpedo-targeting optics were relocated to a column on the centerline in the bridge. From his position, the captain could use voice tubes to speak to the helmsman, radio operator, and motorman. His simple "instrument panel" consisted of three rectangular glass windows through which he could observe a compass and communicate with the wheelhouse interior. A small access port in the rear bulkhead allowed direct contact with the navigator in the chart house, as well as viewing and exchanging charts.

S 26 established the basic form of the wartime Schnellboote but was unique in its two trunk-type engine room ventilators positioned on the centerline, and its four large cabinet-type air vents, carryovers from S 25. Boats after S 26 deleted the cabinet ventilators and added a third trunk ventilator, with two side-by-side on the forward deckhouse, thereby finalizing the ventilator layout that had been the subject of much experimentation. S 27 to S 29 are thus nearly identical in appearance to early S 38 class boats.

In early 1942, three boats of this class – S 26, S 27, and S 28 – were shipped to the Black Sea via Dresden where they were partially disassembled and moved overland to the Danube at Ingolstadt.

S 26 Class (S 26)

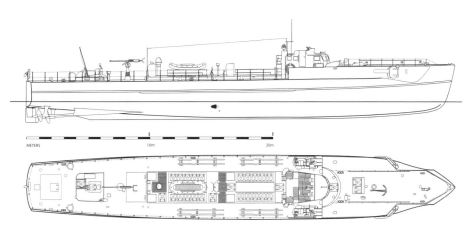

S 26 (left) is berthed alongside S 25 in the Berghaven, Hoek van Holland, Netherlands, in May 1940. The new design enclosed the tubes in a raised forecastle.

This 1940 view from S 26's foredeck shows several characteristics of the S 26 class: a narrow breakwater, two signalman's platforms with tall railings, and a lack of bridge windscreens. The manual anchor winch, seen here under its canvas cover, was also a common feature, but carried over into the first few S 38 boats. Radio aerials are attached to the platform railings. (C. Mucha collection)

An S 30 class vessel assigned to the 3rd "Afrika" Schnellbootsflottille (S-Boot Flotilla) prepares for another mission out of Mersa Matruh, Egypt. This flotilla began operations in the Mediterranean Sea in December 1941. The S 30s performed patrols in support of the Deutsches Afrikakorps (DAK) in North Africa. (R. Mundt collection)

S 61 makes a show of force at the Piazza San Marco in Venice, Italy. It and S 54 limped out of fuel into Venice harbor to demand and receive its surrender to the Germans on 12 September 1943 – four days after Italy's armistice with the Allies. Oblt.z.S. Klaus-Degenhard Schmidt – S 54's Kommandant – bluffing with only 40 men and two boats, negotiated the peaceful surrender of Venice's 10,000-man garrison and several naval vessels. He became Military Governor of Venice and was awarded the Knight's Cross.

S 30 Class (S 30 to S 37; S 54 to S 61)

Built contemporaneously with the more modern S 26 class from 1939 to 1940, these 77-ton boats were intended for the Chinese navy but procured by Germany to meet the Kriegsmarine's urgent wartime requirements. Internally they were similar to the 2nd type S 7 class with MB 502 engines (upgraded to supercharged MB 512s in 1942). They were modernized to integrate the torpedo tubes into the covered forecastle but retained the open bridge in front of the enclosed wheelhouse of the pre-war boats. The bridge of these boats was wet since there was little to obstruct the flow of water from the raised foredeck down into the control position, but distinctive upswept flanges port and starboard of the wheelhouse protected the torpedo crew.

The design of these boats proved advantageous in that they were small enough to navigate the Rhine-Rhône canal system. Beginning in October 1941, they were sent to the Mediterranean in support of the Afrikakorps. There, some were modified with wheelhouse armor and additional weapons such as a 2cm Drehkranzlafette in the bow, a 2cm Drilling (triple mount) amidships, and a 2cm Zwilling (twin mount) aft.

S 30 class boats of the 3rd Flotilla in Riga in the summer of 1941 display variations of the splotch camouflage common to this region and time frame. The boat on the right has a unique wave pattern. (PK Lehmann)

S 30 Class

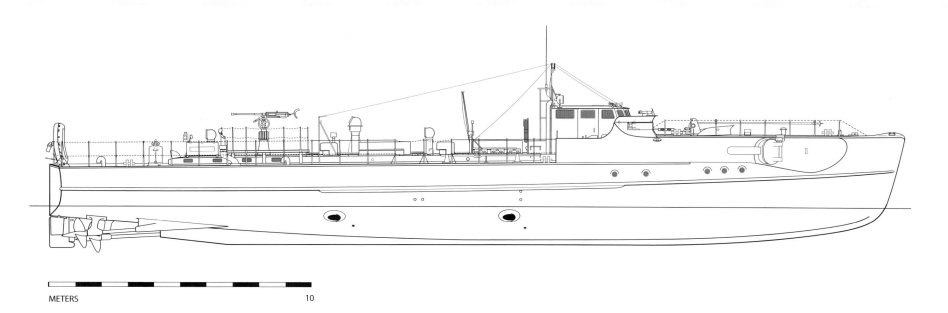

METERS   10

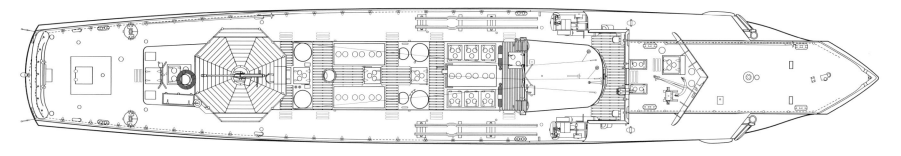

Specifications

Length: .... 32.76 meters
Beam: .... 5.06 meters
Draught: .... 1.47 meters
Displacement: ...... 78.9 tons, 100 tons fully loaded
Powerplant: .... 3 x Daimler Benz MB 502
Speed: .... 36 knots maximum

Range: .... 800 nautical miles
Armament: ..... 2 x 53.3cm torpedo tubes , up to 4 torpedoes.
                1 x 2cm aft, bow pedistal for MG-34
Crew: .... 20 - 22

The "Lürssen Effekt"
(1946 U.S. Navy Technical Report)

"The wing rudders are used to establish the 'Lürssen effect.' These rudders are equipped with levers connected to the main rudder by drag links or rods which cause the rudders to rotate with the main rudders. This effect, only observed at a speed of about 25-28 knots, is based on the flow characteristics in the vicinity of and aft of the propellers. By swinging out the airfoil-shaped side rudders to about 30 degrees, a sudden flow breaking takes place inside the wake and an air-filled hollow space is created so that the direction and acceleration of the water as well as the stern trimming of the vessel is changed.

"The following effects are created:

(a) "The engine revolutions are lowered by about 80 per minute (R.P.M.) or the power rises at constant R.P.M. due to the retained wake. The propeller efficiency is improved, and with engine speed held constant. The ship's speed is increased by one knot.

(b) "The high stern wave ('cock's comb') which lifts at about 10 metres behind the vessel is flattened and the other waves lowered considerably. The stern trim of about 2 degrees at maximum speed is removed so that the vessel runs nearly horizontal.

"The swinging out of the side rudders is done by means of a handwheel in the after engine room at the desired speed and helm angle. As stated above, to establish this effect the wing rudders are moved to an angle of 30 degrees outboard, after which they are swung inward to an angle of approximately 17 degrees to obtain optimum results at speeds of 28 to 40 knots. If the speed of the vessel falls below 20 knots, this effect must be re-established at 28 knots before returning to full speed."

Four S 30 class boats of the Third Flotilla are moored at the Italian navy base at Augusta, Sicily. In the foreground is a freshly maintained S 61. (R. Mundt collection)

S 55 cruises in the Mediterranean. The penguin motif it sports on the upper hull was part of the menagerie of sea creatures identifying individual boats of the 3rd "Afrika" S-Bootsflottille. Some S 30s were retrofitted with a bow-mounted 2cm cannon, which provided additional firepower against enemy aircraft and surface targets. Lürssen built the first eight vessels of this class (S 30 through S 37) for a Chinese order, but the Kriegsmarine commandeered the boats when war broke out in Europe in 1939.

Back from a sortie with members of the Propaganda Kompanie onboard, an S 30 boat of the 2nd Flotilla prepares to dock in the Voorhaven in Ostende, Belgium, 1940. The boat is painted in standard colors, plus an improvised camouflage scheme of random deck gray brush strokes over the upper vertical surfaces. A reserve torpedo is secured under a dark canvas cover. In the background is the Belgian Royal Yacht Club building, comandeered as an upscale billet for U-Boot men. Built in 1906, it still stands.

Members of S 59's crew congregate around an ER2 civil band radio on the aft deck while their boat is moored in the Den Helder Buitenhaven, Netherlands, on 6 May 1941. A life raft is mounted at the stern for crew transfer and evacuation. The 2cm gun is pointed fully vertical while the vessel is in port. Aft torpedo tube doors flank the boat's wheelhouse. The photo is probably taken from the bow of the accommodation ship Hr. Ms. *Konigin Emma* permanently moored here until destroyed by the RAF in 1942. The Dutch locals appear to be curious and friendly.

S 38 Class (S 38 through S 53, S 62 through S 99, S 101 through S 135, and S 137 through S 138)

The S 38 class was a continuation of the S 26 series and the culmination of Lürssen's diligent prewar efforts to design a highly capable, stealthy, and fast fighting boat. Its large displacement – about twice that of Allied PT boats – gave it superior range, endurance, crew protection, versatility, and sea-keeping. It was an innovative design that proved adaptable to a variety of tasks and weapon upgrades, and able to carry out operations effectively even when facing overwhelming Allied air and sea superiority.

Although the early S 38 class boats were very similar to S 27 through S 29, the S 38 class underwent continuous modification on the basis of accumulated front-line experience. In particular, firepower was increased to counter steadily escalating enemy MTB and, particularly, MGB opposition. Like their predecessors, the earliest S 38 boats had a single 2cm Flak in the aft gun position. Beginning in 1941, an additional 2cm Flak in a Scarff ring was mounted into a recess in the forecastle. Typically, this bow gun was retrofit to earlier boats. In many cases, the aft weapon was upgraded from the standard 2cm weapon to a shielded or unshielded 4cm Bofors mounted on a raised wooden platform with folding sides. Depending on crew needed to man the Flak guns, these boats had a complement of about 25 men and an occasional dog. Eleven S 38 units were transported by canal, river, and road to the Black Sea in early 1942.

Three 2,000-horsepower, 20-cylinder Mercedes Benz 501 diesel engines provided the S 38 class boats with ample power for speed and maneuverability. Electrical power was supplied by a pair of 7.5kw 110-volt diesel generators located in the aft engine room.

Experiments with the S 67 attempted to reduce the silhouette through the addition of an 8mm thick clear Plexiglas dome fitted around the bridge and wheelhouse areas, but the material was found to be impractical. Continuing the S 67 experiment, S 68 was given a metal-alloy dome. The design was successful but difficult to produce. Next, a simplified version was manufactured from faceted sheet-metal plates with an armored center section of 10mm-12mm Wotan steel, a front bulkhead of 10mm steel, and a rear one of 8mm steel. Due to increasing casualties sustained by bridge crews, this armored dome, referred to as the "Kalotte" (skull cap), was standardized upon completion of S 100 in May 1943, and the remaining incomplete S 38 class commissioned with an armored Kalotte in place. Beginning in early 1943, a retrofit program equipped front-line boats with the Kalotte, using a parts kit made in Germany and shipped by rail to bases as far as the Black Sea. This modification was not uniform and was made according to the needs of the boats' deployment area. The added weight of the armored bridge reduced speed by about two knots.

The S 38 class was the most produced of all Schnellboot variants. Construction began in early 1940 and continued to the middle of 1943, when the design was superseded by the S 100 class. The numbering sequence of the boats can be misleading, since S 38 class boats 101 to 133 were built between 1940 and 1943 by Schlichting, concurrently with lower numbered boats built by Lürssen.

S 28, seen here in the Black Sea, is practically identical to the early S 38 class boats. Modifications to boats built after S 26 were incorporated into the plans for the lead boat of the next series, thus establishing the S 38 class. S 28 has here been retrofitted with a 2nd type bow 2cm gun. (PK Rolf Kröncke via PT Boats, Inc.)

S 109 moves through the water as sunlight filters through gaps in the cloud cover. It is armed with the first type bow 2cm gun in a simple Scarff ring. (Ferdinand Urbahns)

S 38 Class (S 38 - 53 Series, 1940 - 41, Refit with Bow Gun)

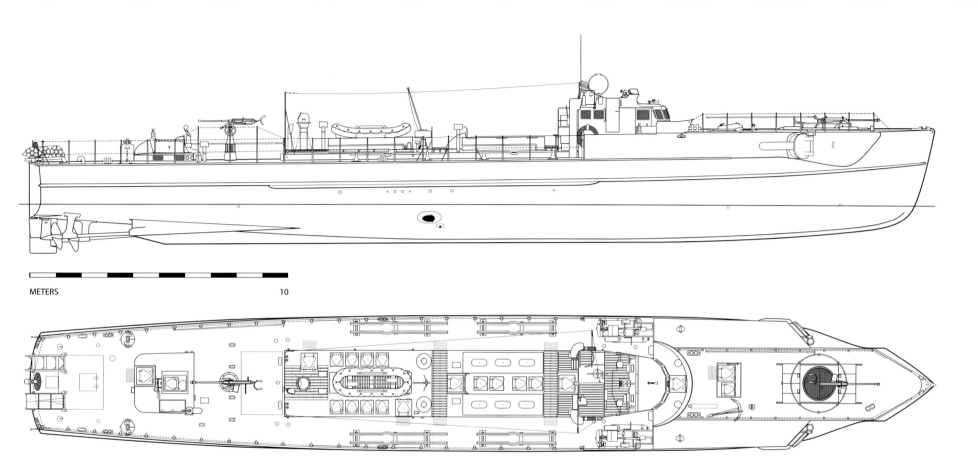

METERS   10

Specifications

Length: .... 34. 94 meters
Beam: .... 5.28 meters
Draught: .... 1.67 meters
Displacement: .... 92.5 tons, 112 tons fully loaded
Powerplant: .... 3 x Daimler Benz MB 501
Speed: .... 39 knots maximum / 35 cruising

Range: .... 700 nautical miles
Armament: ...... 2 x 53.3cm torpedo tubes , up to 4 torpedoes
                       1x 2cm aft, 1 x 2cm in bow turret
Crew: .... 21 - 26

Two early S 38 class boats are moored in the shadow of a harbor wall on the French Channel coast. They are well maintained and have been refit with first type bow guns. The characteristic rectangular sliding covers are seen here open and closed. Cylindrical, French-made smoke buoys are stowed amidships. The boat on the right has very early production features such as a small helmsman's window, a manual anchor winch, and small mushroom ventilators on the foredeck. All of these features were soon phased out of production.

An S 38 class boat on North Sea patrol displays the panther insignia of the 4th S-Bootsflottille and the personal wavy-H emblem of Oblt.z.S Helmut Dross. The captain's initials were often used as boat markings and call signs. (PT Boats, Inc. collection)

Command personnel occupy S 73's open bridge. Radio antenna spreaders are on either side of the bridge, and a UHF radio antenna is located on the starboard side, near the signal light. (E.J. Bakker collection)

This mid-production S 38 class boat has a 4cm Bofors. Assigned to the rear of a formation in a withdrawal, it could effectively discourage enemy pursuit. The circular Kent screen in the helmsman's window appeared early in S 38 production. (H.W. Poppe collection)

(From left) Funker (Radioman) and Rudergänger (Helmsman) stand watch in the wheelhouse of S 105 deployed to Finland. The horn, here facing backwards, swiveled via a hand crank inside the wheelhouse roof. (PK Hugo Bürger)

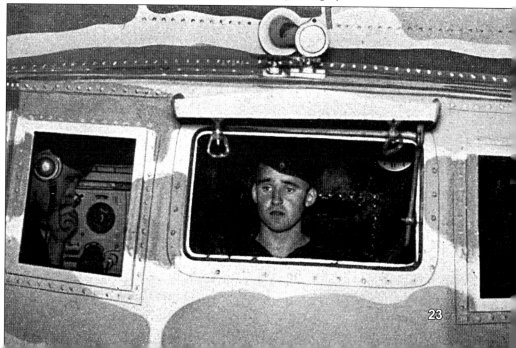

Lt.z.S. Hans-Viktor Howaldt's S 105 replenishes from flotilla tender *Tsingtau* in the Turku Archipelago of southern Finland in 1941. In the absence of shore facilities, tenders would provide the Schnellboote with fuel, torpedoes, ammunition, food, and other supplies, as well as undertake some repairs. This capability meant that Schnellboote deployed to remote locations could extend their time on station. Mounted to the center of the bridge wind deflector is S 105's talisman, a gold painted horseshoe. It appears S 105's radioman is providing music for the work detail via a portable speaker on the chart house roof. (PK Hugo Bürger)

The addition of armor for bridge and wheelhouse crew was another step forward in evolution. Experiments with field fitted armor preceded the standardized armored bridge. The forward half of this wheelhouse is clad in flat metal panels. Window openings are equipped with hinged armored shutters. (J. Klein collection)

A standard S 38 class boat is moored to port of an armored S 38. The latter has the streamlined Kalotte (skull cap) armored bridge, which became standard on this class. This Kalotte enclosed the bridge and wheelhouse areas with steel armor plates ranging in thickness from 8mm to 12mm. (F. Wiemers collection)

A 4cm Bofors armed S 38 class boat is trailed by two Flotilla mates on a daylight sortie. Although presently unmanned, the folding sides of the Bofors platform are lowered, indicating the gun is cleared for action. Just ahead of the gun platform on the starboard side is a Nebelboje 38 smoke buoy. Unlike the boat's fixed smoke generators, the buoy could be thrown overboard to create a stationary / decoy smoke screen.

Increased Allied air and sea superiority in the English Channel called for increased defensive armament. This May 1944 Channel Front photo shows an armored boat fitted with a 2cm Flak Vierling in a 38/43 U mount. Its high rate of fire is evidenced by the three ammunition lockers, with a fourth behind the gun. It is stowed with its four barrels removed and shields folded. This gun, though effective, was not commonly deployed on S-Boote. (PK Rolf Kröncke)

An armored S 38 Schnellboot plows through moderate seas during a daylight patrol. The black number "6" painted on the bow is an identification number within a training Flotilla. Captains of operational boats preferred less impersonal markings. Kriegsmarine S-Boote usually trained in the North and Baltic Seas near the German coast. (PK Rolf Kröncke via PT Boats, Inc. collection)

A wartime censor has overpainted the number "6" on the bow of this armored S 38. This boat is also pictured above and on page 1. The Schnellboot is moving at high speed and the lower bow lifts just above the water. Several crewmen stand watch on the open bridge. (PK Rolf Kröncke via PT Boats, Inc. collection)

An armored S 38 S-Boot is moored at its base in 1943. A 2cm C/38 cannon is mounted in the foredeck, while the open hatchway aft of this weapon provides access to the senior ratings' quarters. The small open hatch immediately forward of the bridge provides light and ventilation to the captain's quarters directly below. Canvas dodgers are placed over the port and starboard railings and a 4cm cannon is located on the afterdeck. (F. Wiemers collection)

Armored S 38 Class (S 91)

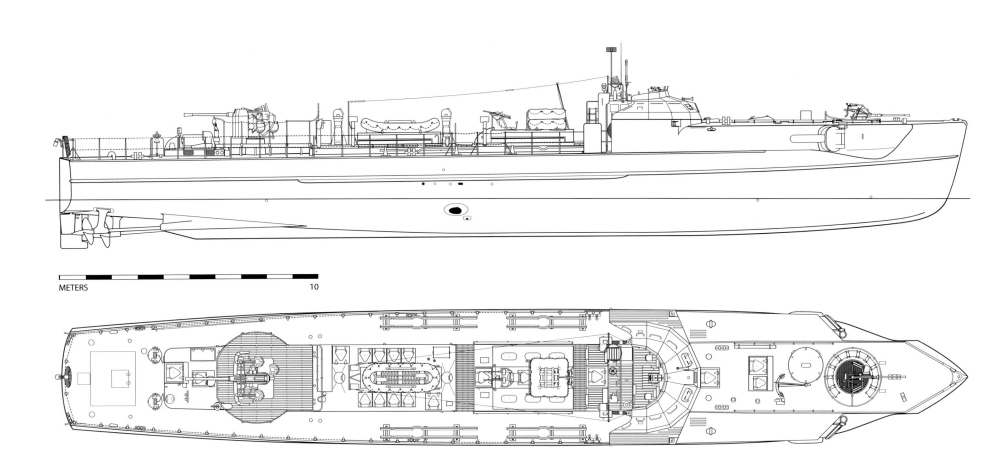

METERS   10

Specifications

Length: .... 34.94 meters
Beam: .... 5.1 meters
Draught: .... 1.5 meters
Displacement: .... 95 tons standard 115 fully loaded
Powerplant: .... 3 x Damlier Benz MB 501
Speed: .... 37 knots maximum / 35 cruising

Range: .... 700 nautical miles
Armament: ...... 2 x 53.3cm torpedo tubes, up to 4 torpedoes.
AA weapons (typical within class):
1x 4cm Bofors aft, 1x 2cm Flak in bow turret
2 x 7.9mm MG15 in "Zwillingssockel" midships,
up to 6 x MG 15 on pintles alongside wheelhouse.
Crew: .... 21 - 30

S 91 wears camouflage for daylight operations in June of 1944. It is unusual to see an armored bridge S-Boot in camouflage or a whimsical ladybug mascot placed on the armored bridge's lantern mount. S 91's Kommandant, Oblt.sZ. Heinz Nolte, stands on the open bridge (third from left). An MG 15 is mounted on either side of the bridge. (E. J. Bakker collection)

Kommandant Kptlt. Walter Knapp's personal insignia – ALTER within a stylized W – is painted on the Kalotte of his armored S 38 vessel. The leaping buck is the emblem of the 8th S-Bootsflottille. (F. Wiemers collection)

S 67's experimental Plexiglas domed wheelhouse was not a success, but the basic form and dimensions were utilized for the armored Kalotte. (Private Collection)

Wheelhouse Armor Development

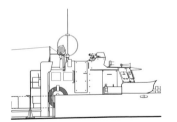

S-38 with Field-Fitted Armor 1942

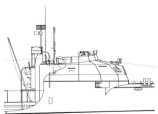

S-67 Experimental Plexiglas Kalotte 1942

S-38 First Type Panzer Kalotte 1943

S-100 Standardized Panzer Kalotte 1944

An armored S 38 Schnellboot plows through the sea on a combat mission. It is armed with one 2cm Flak cannon in the foredeck, a 7.92mm Zwillingsockel (twin mount) 36 machine gun amidships, and another 2cm weapon aft. A gun shield has been installed on the latter gun. Canvas dodgers draped over the railings kept most sea water off the after deck. Horizontal surfaces and the superstructure aft of the bridge were uniformly painted dark gray. Vertical surfaces were finished in the standard Schnellbootweiß. This boat carries two compasses on the aft deckhouses. (PK Rolf Kröncke)

Prior to another winter sortie into the English Channel, all 24 crewmen of this 2nd Flotilla's armored S 38 muster on deck for the Kommandant's instructions. The flotilla's ace of clubs insignia is painted on the side of the hull, below the bridge. Armored S 38 Schnellboote typically had a crew of up to 30 men. This photo affords a view of the bow gun's ready ammunition, stowed in retainers on the deck, as well as the rear of the depression rail, which is raised to prevent the gun being aimed at the wheelhouse and bridge crew. The rectangular object on top of port side ventilator is a housing for a portable, battery powered signal lantern. This lamp had two independent lights, one red and one green. The vertical mast seen starboard and just aft of the bridge cockpit is the night signal mast. It was used for directional IFF signaling and showed two pairs of small lamps, the colors of which could be changed. The port side formation lamp has a visor above and below, to minimize visibility to enemy aircraft. Discrete signal and position lamps such as these, were necessary when deploying flotillas at night and close to the enemy. (PK Rolf Kröncke)

S 100 Class (S 100, S 136, S 139 through S 150, S 167 through S 228, and S 301 through S 305)

Based on intensive combat experience in the English Channel, the 100-ton boat design began commissioning in mid 1943. The S 100 class was a continuation of the S 38, incorporating the armored Kalotte and bow gun tub. The supercharged MB 511 engine was intended to be standard, but due to production shortfalls and delays, some boats completed prior to December 1943 were still equipped with the MB 501.

External features of this class varied greatly as the Kriegsmarine contracted arrangements and secondary armaments for individual boats as required. In general, these boats carried heavier Flak, such as the 3.7cm gun in the aft position and/or a 2cm Zwilling midships. The design was continually economized to make up for strains on production; fittings such as the torpedo cradles were simplified, ventilation hatches were eliminated, and so on. Beginning with S 219, fuel capacity was increased, giving the boats a 750-mile (1,400km) range at 35 knots. These boats had a complement of about 25 men.

Numerous boats ordered in 1944 were not completed by the war's end; numbers 501-699 were reserved for captured boats.

Launching a 53.3cm torpedo from its port tube during a training exercise, S 206 is armed with a shielded 4cm Bofors cannon on the aft deck. S 100s often had an aft-mounted 3.7cm Rheinmetall Flak M 42 in LM 42 or, occasionally, LM 43 U mountings. (PT Boats, Inc. collection)

S 190 departs the Joh. Schlichting boat yard in Travemünde, upon its acceptance by its Kriegsmarine crew, April 1944. The sides, bridge coaming, and probably the stern, are already painted in its 2nd Flotilla marking, an underscored red ace of diamonds. On 23 June 1944, S 190 was scuttled off Normandy after 10.2cm gunfire from British destroyers disabled its engines. Three crewmen were wounded and one was killed.

S 206 cruises at slow speed while on patrol. The open starboard torpedo tube door indicates enemy contact is expected. Each torpedo tube could be reloaded in about two minutes; however, hit-and-run attacks usually precluded such rapid successive reloading. (PT Boats, Inc. collection)

S 205 *Ha-Jü,* still bearing the name of its previous Kommandant, Kptlt. Hans-Jürgen Seeger, was the second 4th Flotilla S 100 class boat to surrender to the Royal Navy at Felixstowe on 13 May 1945. Both boats were built by Lürssen in 1944 and display late-war features. (J. Lambert collection)

Three S-Boote are berthed alongside the flotilla tender *Tanga* in Saßnitz, Pommern, Germany, in April 1944. This and other tenders provided S-Boote with supplies, repairs and crew quarters when they operated away from adequate port facilities. The gun shield in the foreground belongs to S 179's 3.7cm Flak; mounted to the shield is an 8.6cm R Ag M 42 rocket launcher. The camouflaged ship in the background is minelayer *Lothringen.* (Herbert Altpeter)

On 13 May 1945, the S 100 class S 204 *Lang* earned the dubious distinction of being the first Kriegsmarine surface unit to surrender after Germany capitulated. S 204 was assigned to the 4th S-Bootsflottille, whose panther insignia is painted on the side of the hull. While docked at Felixstowe, England, victorious British sailors painted a dagger piercing the panther's neck. (PT Boats, Inc. collection)

British officers on the open bridge help S 204's original crew guide *Lang* into Felixstowe after the surrender. The dark vertical stripe painted on the Kalotte was intended to hide boot scuffs. The S 100 class was designed with the Kalotte as standard, unlike the retrofitted armored bridge of the similar armored S 38 vessels. The cylindrical protrusion on the rear of the chart house is stowage for a portable blinker lamp. (R.W. Brown)

Two Royal Navy officers examine *Lang*. The 2cm bow gun barrel is stowed inside the tube near the foredeck access hatch. (J. Lambert collection)

Repairs begin on S 188 after a 6 June 1944 gunfight with three Canadian corvettes off Normandy left Kommandant Kptlt. Karl-Eberhard Karcher and one crewman wounded.

Late S 100 Class Bridge

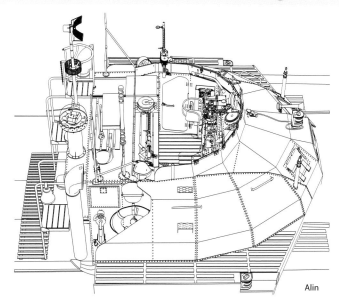

Alin

33

S 100 Class (S 195 - S 218 Series 1944-1945)

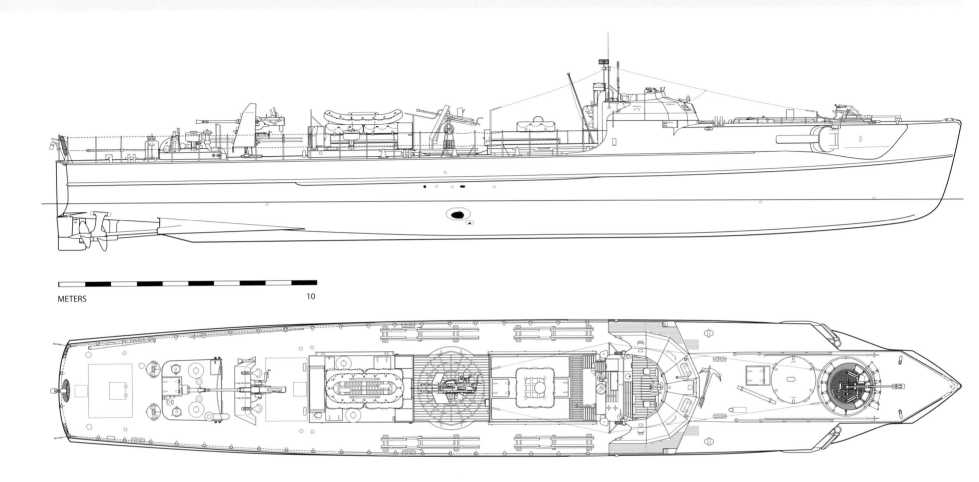

METERS   10

Specifications

Length: .... 34.94 meters

Beam: .... 5.1 meters

Draught: .... 1.5 meters

Displacement: .... 105 tons standard, 122 tons fully loaded

Powerplant: .... 3 x Damlier Benz MB 511

Speed: .... 42 knots maximum / 35 cruising

Range: .... 700 nautical miles

Armament: .... 2 x 53.3cm torpedo tubes, up to 4 torpedoes.
AA weapons: 1x 3.7cm Flak 42, 3 x 20mm Flak.
Up to four 7.92mm MG 15 on pintles alongside wheelhouse
1x 8.6cm R Ag M 42 starshell projector on aft gunshield.

Crew: ....21 - 30

S 204 arrives at Felixstowe for formal surrender, 13 May 1945. The crew is wearing the service dress blue uniform for the occasion, ordinarily they would wear work uniforms while at sea. The bow gun is stowed. (All photos on this page J. Lambert collection)

S 205 (left) and S 204 (right) shortly after surrender. Typically, the boats were built to the same basic design but close comparison will reveal differences. The German crew are taken aboard a Fairmile B motor launch.

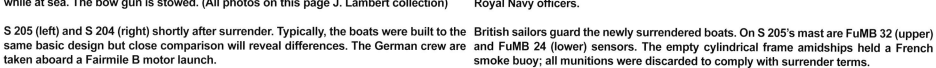

S 204 (middle) S 205 (left) moored alongside their former adversary, a Fairmile D. The boats are occupied by a mix of German crewmen, armed British sentries and curious Royal Navy officers.

British sailors guard the newly surrendered boats. On S 205's mast are FuMB 32 (upper) and FuMB 24 (lower) sensors. The empty cylindrical frame amidships held a French smoke buoy; all munitions were discarded to comply with surrender terms.

With their German crews now in captivity, S 205 (left) and S 204 await their fate. The canvas dodgers are still in place, but S 205's British captors have left the normally orderly and clean decks in disarray. Additional splinter shields were fitted to the sides of the 3.7cm gun on the after deck, and an R Ag M 42 rocket launcher was mounted directly to the armor plate. The life preservers at the stern were issued in solid red but have been decorated with alternating bands of Schnellbootweiß. (J. Lambert collection)

The S 100 class boats, *Ha-Jü* (port) and *Lang* (starboard) are berthed side-by-side after their surrender to British forces in 1945. *Lang's* stern has the monogram TA painted under the comet. Detachable mine rails were fitted to both vessels' afterdecks. These S-Boote laid mines off the Belgian coast during the final weeks of the war. (J. Lambert collection)

Canvas dodgers have been removed from the railings of the S 100 class boat *Ha-Jü* at Felixstowe in May of 1945. Their absence reveals the mine rails located along the sides, and the two cylindrical NA 28 Heck-Nebelanlage (NA 28 stern smoke dischargers) mounted on the after deck. The meaning of the comet and Gothic h painted on the stern are unknown, but probably related to the vessel's radio call sign. (PT Boats, Inc. collection)

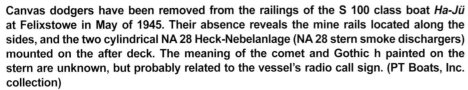

A crane hoists a boat up for lower-hull repairs, The vessel bears the call markings JW and the crest of the 2nd Training Flotilla. It has an unusual combination of two 2cm Zwilling Flak midships (under tarp) and aft. (All photos this page, private collection)

Among the many details of this 2nd Training Flotilla boat are the 4cm gun's Bosch siren which transmitted open fire/cease fire commands from the bridge, racks for gun crew helmets on the depression rail, and an extra ammunition box elevated for clearance over the engine room hatches.

Officers and men of the 2nd Training Flotilla enjoy ideal conditions on the Baltic in 1944. By 1945 the collapsing German front forced the flotilla into combat operations. The removable bow lantern is attached to its mount and plugged into the electrical outlet.

This 2nd Training Flotilla boat is equipped with a windowless, KM 20 Mutterkompaß (master gyro compass) part of the PFK (S) 43 set which fed data to repeater compasses in the navigator's cabin, wheelhouse and bridge. This was used on Kalotte bridge boats, due to the armor plate interfering with magnetic compasses.

S 151 Class (S 151 through S 158)

The S 151 class was a unique class of boat, designed by Lürssen for the Bulgarian Navy, built at the Gusto Werke in Schiedam, the Netherlands, under German occupation, and commissioned into the Kriegsmarine. Gusto had been contracted to license build British Power Boat designed MTBs for the Dutch Navy, but upon the Dutch capitulation in 1940, Gusto was pressed into German service. These boats were fitted out with standard Kriegsmarine 53.3cm torpedo tubes and a 2cm Flak. At 28.3m in length and 4.46m beam, these were also able to navigate the narrow European canal system and were thus deployed to the Mediterranean. Field modifications included armor plate over the wheelhouses and additional light anti-aircraft weapons, including the 2cm Drilling.

S 700 Class (S 701 through S 709)

Based on experiments with the S 226, in 1944 a new design was proposed for a boat carrying two rear firing tubes and a 3cm bow gun as standard equipment. Loaded with sound homing "Zaunkönig" torpedoes, the rear tubes were intended as defense against enemy pursuit. However, with the cancellation of the specified MB 518 motor necessary for the seven-ton increase, the S 700 design proposals were abandoned in favor of producing additional boats built to standard S 100 plans. Likewise, plans for a "Panzerboot," an armored gunboat version of the S-Boot, were cancelled. S 701 - S 709 were built by Danziger Waggonfabrik as standard late-war S 100 types.

S 700 Class (planned)

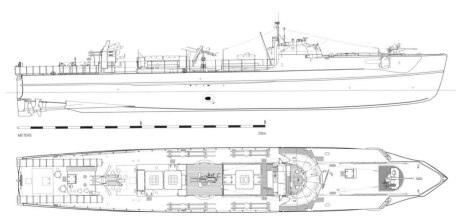

An S 151 class Schnellboot slowly cruises past a Luftwaffe seaplane hangar in Swinemünde. This class of small vessel was originally designed by Lürssen for the Bulgarian navy but license built in Holland and taken into the Kriegsmarine. A Dutch boatyard completed eight S 151 class S-Boote between 1941 and 1942. The hangar still exists. (PT Boats, Inc. collection)

A pair of S 151 class vessels patrol off German-occupied Sardinia. These S-Boote were small enough to navigate the narrow Rhine/Rhône canal system, which led from the North Sea to the Mediterranean. The S 151s were deployed as the 7th Flotilla, which fought alongside the 3rd Flotilla in support of the DAK, engaged in fighting Allied forces in North Africa. (PT Boats, Inc.collection)

This unidentified S 151 boat of the 7th Flotilla bears a unique crossbow and heraldic shield insignia. The compact deck layout called for a double door to the bridge, due to lack of clearance. The coiled heavy rope on the side of the gun platform aft of the bridge offered some splinter protection.

On patrol in support of the Afrikakorps, an Oberbootsmaat / leichte Flak Geschützführer (Petty Officer / AA gun captain) on S 157's signal platform and his crewmates keep a lookout. The boat's Kommandant, Oblt.z.See Heckel, can be identified by his white cap. Interior spaces lacked adequate ventilation for warm climes. (R. Mundt collection)

A G7a torpedo with six bladed props is loaded onto an S 151 boat of the 7th Flotilla. The 2cm Flak in the aft gun position has been upgraded to a dual mount. The doubled ammunition consumption has led to a field-added ammunition locker on the port side. The storage box bridging the lockers probably contains spare parts for the guns, or an optical rangefinder. The tube over it is a spare 2cm barrel container. The Kommandant, identified by his white cap, and First Officer appear to be wearing the "U-Boot Päckschen," the gray-green, denim battledress favored by U-Boot crews. (R. Mundt collection)

Crewmen paint the deckhouses, having first removed wooden walkways in preparation. The view aft shows the compact deck layout and two reserve torpedoes. The trunk ventilators over the engines are fitted with extra cowl ventilators in place of the forward portholes. With exception of the wheelhouse arrangement, the S 151 class shared many design characteristics of the S 30 class.

The "W" insignia visible in this photograph taken in Augusta, Italy, in 1943, identifies this shrapnel-damaged vessel as the 7th Flotilla's S 155, which was under the command of Kptlt. Wolf Dietrich Babbel.

The RZA binocular torpedo sight, voice pipe, and windshields are visible in this cockpit. A brass "W" insignia is the crew's unofficial cap badge. A popular morale booster with U-Boot men, such badges were uncommon among Schnellboot crews.

Allied air superiority forced the Germans to undertake numerous countermeasures. Here S 155 has been field fitted with a platform for a twin MG 15 aft of the wheelhouse, one of many *ad hoc* schemes to increase firepower of this class. By 1944, Flak armament was increased on some 151 class boats to five 20mm guns, plus rudimentary wheelhouse armor. A torpedo pistol container is on the wheelhouse platform.

S 151 Class

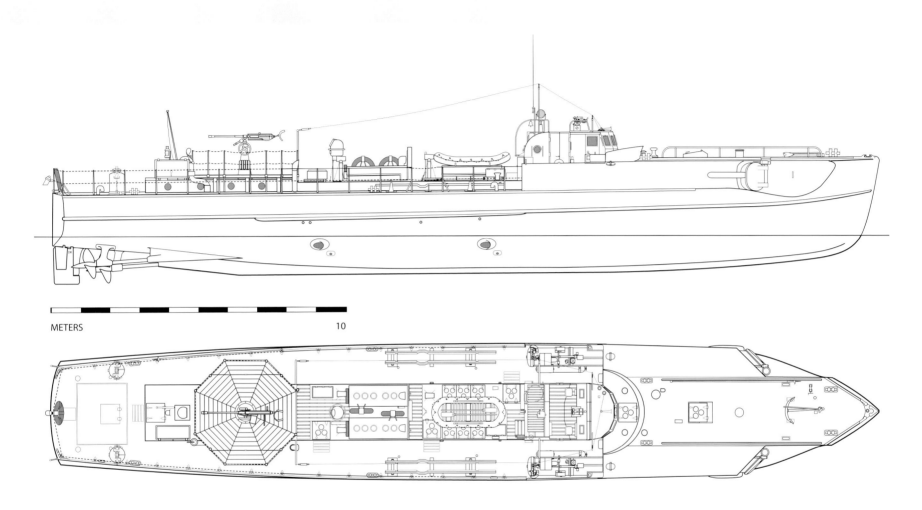

METERS   10

Specifications

Length: .... 28.3 meters
Beam: .... 4.46 meters
Draught: .... 1.42 meters
Displacement: .... 54 tons standard /68 Fully Loaded
Powerplant: .... 3 x Damlier Benz MB 500
Speed: .... 35 knots maximum / 30 cruising

Range: .... 350 nautical miles
Armament: ...... 2 x 53.3cm torpedo tubes , up to 4 torpedoes.
                  1 x 2cm Flak.
Crew: .... 20 - 22

Leichte Schnellboote (LS 1 through LS 12)

In 1936 the Kriegsmarine began designing a "midget" torpedo boat to be carried aboard surface ships and U-Boote. The concept focused on clandestine deployment within range of distant harbors, where the boats would fire torpedoes or lay mines and then escape. In 1938 work began on the Leichtes Schnellboot (LS) series, of which 34 were planned but 12 completed. The boats were 12.5m long, 3.46m wide, weighed about 11.5 tons, and were to be powered by two Daimler-Benz 850 h.p. MB 507 engines. Berlin's Naglo boatyard built LS 1 from mahogany; the rest were built from light metal by Dornier, specialists in seaplane construction. The LS-Boote were to be armed with two 45cm torpedoes and carry one 20mm Flak in a Plexiglas-domed turret over the wheelhouse.

Due to delays and shortfalls in delivery of engines, turrets, and torpedo tubes, LS 4 was the only boat to meet all original specifications. Nicknamed *Esau,* LS 4 was a great success and could make 42.5 knots. Under the command of Kaptlt. Malte von Schack, LS 4 deployed from auxiliary cruiser *Michel* and sank an impressive 11 Allied merchant ships totaling 79,024 tons.

LS 2 was armed with a 7.9mm MG 34 machine gun in a simple Scarff ring. LS 3 and boats after LS 4 were armed with a 15mm machine gun in turrets of Luftwaffe origin, such as the HD/151/1A. LS 2, 3, 5, and 6 were fitted out as minelayers. Only LS 3 and 4 were powered with MB 507 engines; the rest had troublesome 700 h.p. Junkers Jumo 205 aircraft engines. LS 2 and 3 shipped aboard auxiliary cruisers *Komet* and *Kormoran.* The remaining boats served mainly in the Aegean and Adriatic. Plans to stow LS boats onboard a submarine were never realized.

LS-4 "Esau"

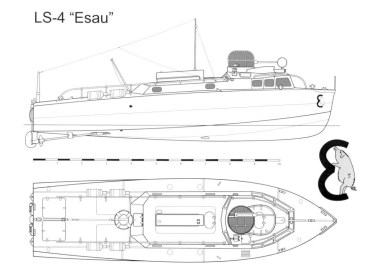

Crewmen aboard the Hilfskreuzer (HK; Auxilliary Cruiser) Komet hoist LS 2 from its hold forward of the bridge structure. This boat was one of three Leichte Schnellboote deployed aboard German auxiliary cruisers. HK Komet and 10 other such vessels were armed merchant ships engaged in raiding Allied cargo vessels throughout the world's oceans. (G. Huff collection)

The profile of LS 3 during its trials shows its 15mm MK 151 gun in a hydraulically operated, Plexiglas-enclosed gun turret. This compact Luftwaffe turret was a practical weapon for a small, lightweight craft. The pennant displays the corporate logo of Dornier, the boat's manufacturer. Dornier, located in Friedrichshafen on the Bodensee (Lake Constance), was a specialist in all-metal seaplane construction, uniquely qualified to build a light but powerful attack craft.

LS 2 *Meteorit's* eight crewmen prepare it for a mission. The LS, painted an overall dark gray, is lowered by crane from *Komet* into the water. LS 2's pair of 700 h.p. Junkers Jumo engines proved unreliable and the boat was eventually scuttled in the Bismarck Archipelago, northeast of New Guinea. *Komet* – formerly the merchant ship *Ems* – was sunk in the English Channel off Cherbourg by the British Motor Torpedo Boat MTB-236 on 14 October 1942. There were no survivors. (G. Huff collection)

LS 2, appropriately nicknamed *Meteorit,* is suspended on *Komet's* derrick between missions. The helmsman's circular window spun at high speed to throw off spray and rain. *Komet's* Arado Ar 196 floatplane is directly behind LS 2. (G. Huff collection)

The unavailability of special torpedo tubes resulted in LS 2 fitting out as a high-speed clandestine minelayer. Three TMB-II magnetic mines were deposited through chutes mounted in the stern. (G.Huff collection)

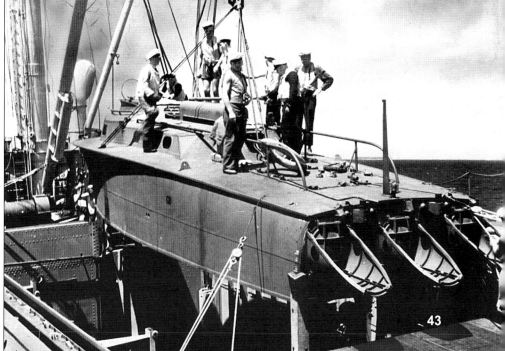

Engines

The large, highly capable Schnellboot was only made possible through the development of an extremely powerful, compact, robust, and relatively lightweight power plant. The Schnellboot engine, like the boats themselves, underwent a constant evolutionary process, in which quality and survivability were prioritized over quantity. As the boats were adapted to operate in increasingly harsh combat environments, improvements in engine performance were necessary to counter the growing weight of armor protection, anti-aircraft weaponry, and additional crewmen. Despite the increasing displacement of the boats, the top speed of the final versions of the Schnellboot exceeded the top speed of the pre-war boats, while fuel consumption remained nearly constant. The motor used in S 1 produced 900 h.p.; the final production type produced a Herculean 2,500 h.p. A 3,000 h.p. engine for S-Boote was in the final stages of development when Germany capitulated, and work had begun on a yet more powerful turbine engine.

As part of the S-Boot development program in the early 1930s, the Kriegsmarine commissioned MAN and Daimler-Benz to build special lightweight high-speed diesels. An important innovation in MTB design, diesel engines reduced both fire risk and fuel consumption. MAN focused on an in-line design and Daimler-Benz on a more compact "V" engine. Both firms used as a basis the powerful, lightweight engine designs developed for Zeppelins during the First World War.

MAN was the first to deliver a production-ready engine. The L7 Zn 19/30 was a seven-cylinder, in-line, double-acting, two-stroke, non-reversing engine. First installed aboard the S 6 to S 9, it produced 1,320 h.p. but its weight exceeded specifications and the boats' maximum speed was only 32 knots. MAN next produced the L11/Zu, a more powerful in-line, four-stroke engine with 11 cylinders producing 2,050 h.p. The engine, larger and heavier than the previous variant, required increasing the dimensions of the S-Boot design. Although they met speed requirements and exceeded the horsepower of the contemporary Daimler-Benz engine, the in-line MAN motors were big, heavy, and tended to suffer from mechanical problems. The long crankshaft was prone to damage through torsion, and the tall casing's high center of gravity put stress on the motor mounts during maneuvers, eventually cracking them.

Concurrently, Daimler-Benz developed a lighter, more compact diesel engine, the MB 502. The first variant, a 16-cylinder V four-stroke engine, produced a maximum of 1,320 h.p. and was more reliable, lighter and consumed less fuel than the MAN L7. Its exhaust gasses were nearly invisible, unlike the dark fumes of the MAN motor. The eventual addition of superchargers to the MB 502 (redesignated MB 512) raised maximum output to 1,650 h.p. S 10 to S 13 with MB 502 engines performed flawlessly in high-speed endurance runs in the Baltic and North Sea, while MAN engine boats proved unreliable and, on-average, slower. These trials convinced naval planners against further use of MAN engines and Daimler-Benz became the single supplier. Daimler-Benz was already heavily engaged in producing aircraft engines and ultimately engine shortages became a critical bottleneck in Schnellboot production, despite exhaustive efforts by factory workers.

Daimler-Benz immediately set about improving the MB 502 / 512 and the result was

A Schnellboot Fahrmaat (motorman) sits by the port engine. His left hand engages the starting lever and his right hand is moving the throttle based on orders from the bridge, which were received on the telegraph to his right, and via lamps on the instrument panel. These engine commands had to be followed immediately lest a collision occur. The small hand wheel between the two levers controls fine speed adjustments. The Fahrmaat wears a black leather protective suit and a life jacket. (PK Hugo Bürger)

the MB 501, a 20-cylinder 2,000 h.p. V engine. Trials with the MB 501 in S 18 - S 25 impressed the Naval Staff and in 1938 they decided upon it as the standard S-Boot motor. The MB 501 proved highly dependable and a versatile basis for later improvements such as the addition of a motor-driven supercharger, which boosted output to 2,500 h.p. The supercharged motor was redesignated MB 511. With a total output of 7,500 h.p., the three MB 511 powering an S 100 class boat with reduced payload could propel it to a record-breaking top speed of approximately 43 knots.

The 3,000 h.p. MB 518 was a final wartime attempt to increase engine output. Tests began in October 1942 with very satisfactory results. However, minor developmental problems coupled with heavy air-raid damage to the factory led to the cancellation of the MB 518 program in favor of additional MB 511 engines.

The Schnellboot's two engine rooms reflected thorough German planning and the smart design inherent in the entire S-Boot program. Although noisy while the engines ran, they were spacious and well ventilated. Prior to economy measures beginning in 1944, engine rooms were well illuminated by skylights. Conduits and wiring were neatly laid out and color-coded to allow accessibility and quick identification for repair. The risk of fire was greatly diminished by the use of diesel fuel and by a built-in Ardex fire extinguishing system. Modern instrument panels displayed performance of the three engines. Instructions from the bridge were received on compact engine order telegraphs and blinker lamps. Although the engines were technological marvels, they required a skilled crew, careful maintenance, and regular overhauls.

Leitender Maschinist (chief engineer) StObMasch. Georg Laue (left) and his men are at their posts in S 105's aft engine room while the middle MB 501 runs. These powerful engines demanded constant attention and careful maintenance. (PK Hugo Bürger)

The 20-cylinder MB 511 engine, seen here, was essentially an MB 501 with the addition of a supercharger. This 2,500-horsepower engine was the penultimate in a series of increasingly powerful diesel boat motors produced by Mercedes during WW2, as they sought to keep pace with Schnellboot development.

A U.S. Navy technician examines a MB 511's supercharger air intake on a captured S-Boot. Ambient air was drawn from the engine room and replenished through ventilators on deck. Exhaust could be vented above water, or below water for muffling. (B. Marshall/U.S. National Archives)

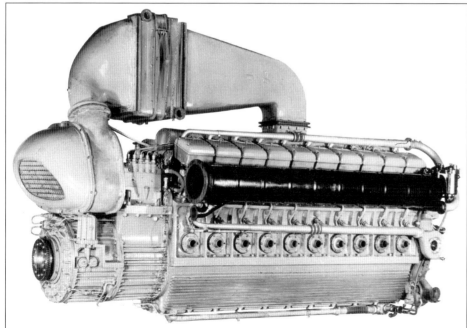

An Obermaschinenmaat (Machinist's Mate 2nd Class) supervises a mechanic while the latter services the MB 501 engine's fuel injector. Maintenance could be a matter of life or death and was emphasized aboard the Schnellboote. Major repairs were undertaken at shore bases or by S-Boot tenders, but crews had to perform routine maintenance themselves at sea. The mechanic wears off-white coveralls, while the petty officer wears a dark navy-blue pea jacket. (PK Warnke)

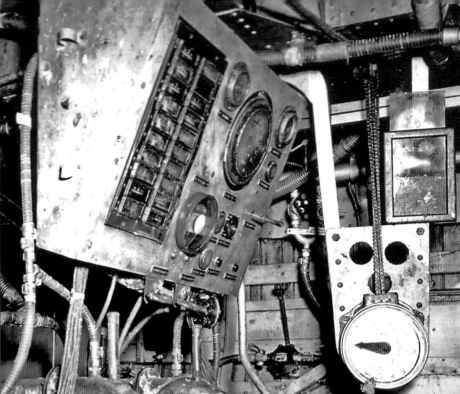

An instrument panel and telegraph relayed information to the motorman. (B. Marshall/ U.S. National Archives)

Below the waterline, engine exhaust passed through the large streamlined vent; the smaller opening provided engine cooling water. (B. Marshall/U.S. National Archives)

Construction

Large and robust, wartime boats were built to withstand considerable stresses of high-speed warfare at sea, long-range fuel capacity and an increasingly heavy weapons load. A combination of wood and metal was used to maximize strength and ease of repair, while minimizing weight. Boat construction took place primarily at Lürssen boatyard in Vegesack near Bremen; many boats were also built by the Schlichting yard in Travemünde, and several were built at the Gusto Werke in Schiedam, Netherlands, and at Danziger Waggonfabrik, Danzig. During the war years, German boatyards completed an average of only approximately three S-Boote per month. While Allied boats may have been considered mass-produced expendibles, the investment of time, material, and meticulous workmanship underscored the Kriegsmarine's concept of the Schnellboot as a strategic asset.

Hull construction began with a heavy oak keel. Longitudinals of pine were bolted to light aluminum alloy transverse frames, spaced at intervals of 575mm. Oak stringers were used for strength around the bow and motor mounts and on the stern. Later boats added aluminum-alloy stringers for additional strength. Bulkheads were designed to withstand flooding and light splinter damage. To save weight they were made of 3mm-thick steel plate from keel to 30cm above the waterline and 4mm-thick aluminum alloy from this point upwards, or all aluminum alloy, braced and stiffened. The collision bulkhead at frame 57 was made of 3mm galvanized steel. Motor mounts were 4mm steel. S 26 and later boats received additional deck bracing to support the Flak guns, as well as aluminum-alloy diagonals to stiffen the frames at bow and stern.

Decks were 23 x 90mm Oregon pine planks over 40mm x 35mm oak timbers spaced 200mm apart. Planks were planed smooth, covered with canvas, and coated with durable synthetic resin paint. Hull planking comprised a 12mm inner layer of either cedar or larch and a 21mm outer layer of mahogany, with muslin between. Along the keel was a single layer of 33mm oak planking. Beginning with S 205, a third planking layer was added to cope with additional weight. Superstructure was constructed of 2.5mm aluminum alloy riveted to 3mm- to 4mm-thick frames of the same material.

The loss of numerous Schnellboote to collisions is more indicative of the darkness and close quarters in which they fought than of any design weakness. This reality was dramatically illustrated by a ramming incident involving S 33 under command of Hans Schultze-Jena in the Skaggerrak on the night of 9-10 May 1940. Lying in a fog bank after a successful attack on HMS *Kelly*, S 33 was suddenly struck by HMS *Bulldog* and then by *Kelly*, under tow by *Bulldog*. A nine-meter section of S 33's bow was torn away, flooding compartments VIII and IX. The severe jolt stalled the engines, stopping the boat about 60 meters astern of two angry destroyers. Whether by flooding or enemy fire, the crew expected to lose their boat and prepared to abandon ship, but the remaining bulkheads held fast and the British destroyers steamed on in the belief the "E-Boat" had not survived. With its bilge pumps straining against the flood of water from numerous holes, the boat returned 200 miles to its base in Wilhelmshaven. S 33 soon returned to battle and soldiered on until 1945, proving the integrity of the Schnellboot design.

At the Schlichting boatyard in Travemünde, workers pause for a brief ceremony to commemorate the launch of S 127 in July 1943. Aluminum alloy diesel fuel tanks (one 1,450-liter and two 3,150-liter) painted light gray, await installment. The small "Effekt" rudders, flanking the main rudder, and the wedge form are visible on the stern. Anti-fouling red is painted beneath the waterline. (PK Vörlander)

The U.S. Naval Intelligence Mission in Europe examined S 144, raised from the harbor basin at Le Havre, France, in April of 1945. The team photographed the vessel and wrote notes about the boat's construction materials directly on their picture. The U.S. Navy never identified this captured vessel with a hull number; instead, they designated it "Captured Enemy Equipment 6527." (B. Marshall/U.S. National Archives)

47

Main Armament

Thomas Whitehead's 1866 invention of the torpedo brought about a revolution in naval warfare. The first torpedoes were short ranged and ponderously slow but their implications were great: the torpedo could enable a small craft to destroy a much larger one, or a small navy to threaten a great navy. Uniquely, it could be aimed and fired underwater. In the naval arms race that preceded the First World War the potential of such a device was appreciated by German naval engineers seeking ways to undermine the British navy's global domination. The German U-Boot fleet, while not securing a victory for Germany in the 1914-1918 war, proved beyond any doubt the effectiveness of Whitehead's invention. During the build up to the Second World War, German naval command again turned to the torpedo, and stealthy delivery systems, such as the S-Boote and U-Boote, as potential equalizers.

The Schnellboot's "main battery" consisted of two specially designed 53.3cm torpedo tubes mounted on the bow. The tubes were electrically heated to prevent ice jamming, and to maintain the torpedo guidance mechanism within operating temperature. Tubes could be fired either by compressed air or explosive charge. Boats typically went into action with one torpedo in each tube, although a reserve load of two additional torpedoes could be carried in cradles aft of the tubes, which a well-trained crew could reload in approximately two minutes.

The G7a, the standard German torpedo of World War II, entered service in 1938. It carried a 300kg Hexanite warhead at speeds up to 44 knots, powered by a Decalene (alcohol) and compressed air fueled turbine. Although its maximum range exceeded 12,000 meters, it was typically fired by S-Boote at ranges of 3,000 meters or less. Its course could be preset for any angle up to 90° from launch. The detonator was either a contact or magnetic influence type. In parallel to the severe problems experienced by the U.S. Navy, the German torpedoes also suffered from unreliable detonators, and no adequate solution was found until late in 1942. The G7a's high-speed setting also proved problematic until middle of the war.

Beginning in June 1944, S-Boote operating in the Channel region deployed the electric powered T3d Dackel and T5a Zaunkönig torpedoes against the Allied supply ships off Normandy, with occasional success. The Dackel's extremely long range of 57,000 meters at 9 knots enabled it to be fired from outside the Allies' defensive line into an anchorage where it would then travel in a pre-set pattern. The Zaunkönig was a fairly effective acoustic homing torpedo modified for S-Boot use with an 8,000-meter range at 22 knots.

Torpedoes were aimed using an optical/mechanical calculating sight. A monocular RZA 2 torpedo targeting sight was mounted on the rear of the wheelhouse roof of the first few boats. Beginning in 1935, these sights were replaced by the RZA 3, a binocular sight with a supplemental Revi (Reflexvisier, or reflector sight) and analog targeting computer. These were mounted on a pedestal in the bridge, on or near the boat's centerline. The improved RZA 5, was introduced in 1937. An improved targeting computer saw use in the mid- to late-war period. Heading was entered by aiming the binoculars at the target while speed and range were entered using hand wheels. The computer calculated a firing solution and relayed settings to the torpedoes. Red lamps in the reticle indicated when the boat reached the firing position. The torpedoes could be fired, either remotely from an electric trigger on the pedestal, or locally by pressing a plunger on the tube.

Flotilla Tender *Tsingtau* lowers a torpedo onto an early S 38 class Schnellboot with the 2nd Flotilla in southwest Finland. Reload rails were mounted aft of each torpedo tube. A tarpaulin covers the aft torpedo tube door. S-Boote normally carried two torpedoes in their tubes and occasionally two in reserve. The cylindrical object midships is a French made smoke buoy in its tripod holder. (PK Hugo Bürger)

Crewmen aboard S 27 in Cherbourg in 1940 gently lower a torpedo onto its cradle. This vessel is equipped with an intermediate type of fixed cradle, which was further simplified on the later S 100 class. The earliest cradle designs stowed the torpedo flush against the deckhouses, increasing deck access. (PK Böltz)

Three Torpedomechaniker (Torpedo Engineers) perform routine maintenance on two 'eels' intended for S-Boot use. Torpedo reliability was always a critical issue and much of it depended on constant maintenance. Contra-rotating propellers within the tail unit provided thrust for the torpedo. (PT Boats, Inc. collection)

An S 30 class boat reloads its torpedoes at a North African base in July 1942. Loading torpedoes was always a delicate operation, due to the torpedoes' fragile gyroscopic guidance mechanism. This mechanism was located in the torpedo's after body and steered the weapon by adjusting the tailfins surrounding the propellers. (PK Pietzsch)

On an S 38 class boat a Torpedomechaniker makes a final inspection of the G7 torpedo loaded in the No. 2 tube. The propellers are four-blade configuration. During freezing weather, the tube's internal electric heating system kept the torpedo's guidance system within operating temperature and prevented ice from jamming the torpedo or the bow doors. The crewman wears a cold-climate black leather work uniform and a fur cap. While at sea, he wears a mid war yellow inflatable life vest over his jacket.

Crewmates look on as a Torpedomechaniker on S 105 refills lubricating oil. To his left and aft of the open tube door is a pintle for a light machine gun. These crewmen are dressed in the standard Kriegsmarine warm climate work uniform consisting of plain reed green cotton jackets and trousers, and dark navy blue wool overseas caps. The boat is camouflaged in a splotch pattern over Schnellbootweiß. The decks and upper surfaces of the torpedo tube are painted dark gray. (PK Hugo Bürger)

Torpedo Tube, Mid Production and G7a Torpedo

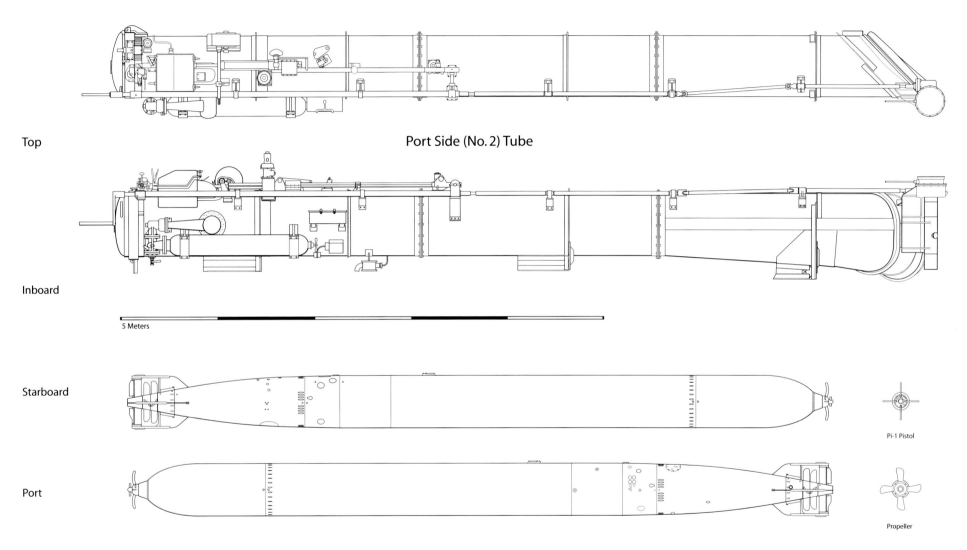

Top

Port Side (No. 2) Tube

Inboard

5 Meters

Starboard

Pi-1 Pistol

Port

Propeller

Length Including Warhead: 7.179 meters
Diameter: 533mm
Weight: 1,532kg
Maximum Horsepower: 300
Explosive Charge: 300kg

Ranges:
6,000 meters at 44 knots
8,000 meters at 40 knots
12,500 meters at 30 knots

Manufacturers:
Deutsche Werke Kiel, Julius Pintsch Berlin, Auto-Union Zwickau, Borgward Bremen, Planeta Dresden.

A torpedoman stands at his battle station aft of the Number Two (port) tube. He is turning the handle that operates the bow torpedo door. The door, opened when enemy contact was expected, was normally kept shut to keep seawater out of the tube. The drum on the outboard side of the tube is the cable reel for the torpedo loading tackle. (PK Waske)

S 105's torpedoman awaits the firing order at the Number Two tube. His right hand rests on the plunger that fires compressed air into the tube from the tank mounted to starboard, forcing the torpedo out. Centered on the tube's door is the circular nameplate of its maker, Julius Pintsch, Berlin. A censor obscured the lettering. (PK Hugo Bürger)

A U.S. Navy sailor examines the port torpedo tube of the salvaged S 144, whose bridge is dismantled. Behind him are the remains of the wheelhouse tachometers, engine order telegraph, and wheel. The aft torpedo tube door sealed by rotating a locking ring. The ring's removable hand crank fit into a gear shaft at the breech's 11 o'clock position. Ammunition canisters for 7.92mm MG 15 machine guns were stowed on the forward bulkhead rack, just to starboard of the tube. (B. Marshall/U.S. National Archives)

Immediately before getting under way, the "Mixer" (Kriegsmarine slang for torpedoman) climbs into S 105's starboard tube to insert the pistol (trigger and detonator unit) into the torpedo's warhead. Once the torpedo was launched, a small propeller attached to the pistol would spin as the torpedo raced through the water, arming the weapon when it reached a safe distance. The empty canister that held the pistol is standing upright on the foredeck, just aft of the anchor. (PK Hugo Bürger)

G7a Torpedo Colors and Markings

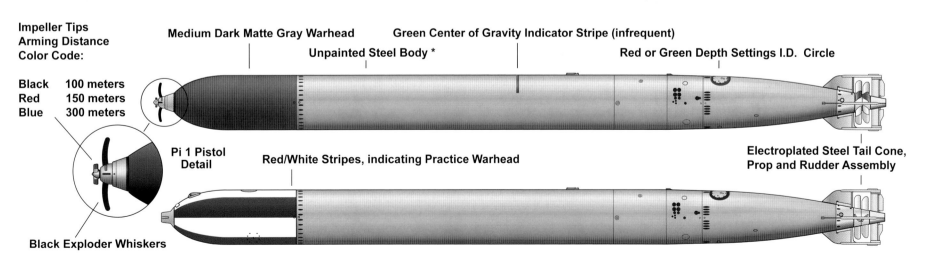

Impeller Tips
Arming Distance
Color Code:

Medium Dark Matte Gray Warhead
Unpainted Steel Body *
Green Center of Gravity Indicator Stripe (infrequent)
Red or Green Depth Settings I.D. Circle

Black   100 meters
Red   150 meters
Blue   300 meters

Pi 1 Pistol Detail
Red/White Stripes, indicating Practice Warhead
Electroplated Steel Tail Cone, Prop and Rudder Assembly

Black Exploder Whiskers

* A wax-based rust inhibitor was routinely field-applied to the steel.

RZA 5 auf SZS 1a

The RZA 5 torpedo sight is mounted at the center of the bridge of the S 100 class boat *Ha-Jü*. A round, dark ventilator cover hangs on the side of the bridge, immediately above a life ring holder. This S-Boot was field modified to include a helmet rack and additional voice pipes to below decks positions. A machine gun pintle and an oval hand grip are located on the Kalotte's starboard aft edge. (J. Lambert collection)

The RZA 5 torpedo sight is located directly aft of the bridge compass. Flexible voice tubes enabled communication to various points within the boat. The two rectangular ports provided direct communication with the wheelhouse crew.

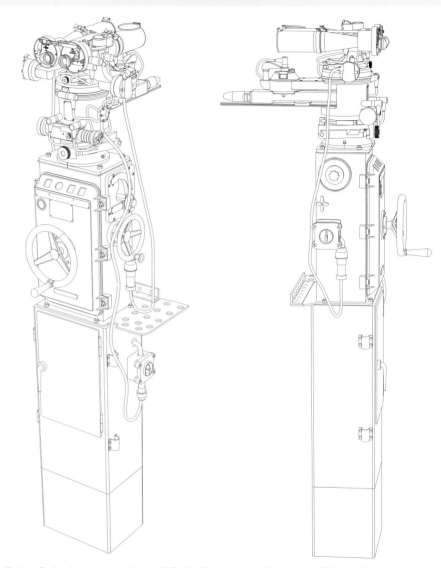

The Zeiss Rohrzielapparat 5 mit D.F. 7x50 H und Reflexvisier (RZA 5 Torpedo Sight, with 7x50 Binocular and Reflex Sight) is fitted on its Hagenuk Schnellboot Zielsäule 1a (SZS 1a Schnellboot Targeting Column) analog computer. The SZS 1a appeared in 1943, making this the final wartime version of the torpedo sight. The combination was a compact, accurate, and easily operated day/night targeting system, ideal for S-Boot use. Although Zeiss designed the RZA 5 in 1937, a nearly identical version was still in use with the post war Bundesmarine, until rendered obsolete by guided torpedoes.

Secondary Armament

As the war progressed, the Schnellboote were forced to defend themselves against ever stronger Allied countermeasures, including growing air superiority and British Motor Gunboats (MGBs) built specially to combat the German "E-boat" threat. In addition to armor plate introduced with the S 38 class, firepower increased as per Schnellboot fleet Commander F.Kpt. Rudolf Petersen's observation: "In Schnellboot battles, the maximum amount of iron should be fired at the enemy as quickly as possible."

For close defense, covering boarding parties etc., early boats carried one or two WWI-vintage 7.92mm MG08/15 water-cooled machine guns. This armament was later upgraded to the MG34 light machine gun. Two or three MG34 were carried in the boat's weapons' locker and could be mounted on pintles at the bow and beside the wheelhouse. Many armored S 38 class boats were fitted with the Zwillingsockel 36, which mounted two MG34 or MG15 light machine guns in a manually-operated anti-aircraft turret. Its advantages were light weight, minimal crew requirement, and small size, enabling it to fit between the ventilators above the forward engine room. Later in the war, the 7.92mm MG15 saw widespread use on S-Boote, usually mounted on pintles to either side of the bridge. Other light munitions included MP-40 submachine guns for boarding parties, hand grenades and signal flares.

As its standard anti-aircraft gun, the S-Boote first carried a single 2cm Rheinmetall MG C/30 cannon on a platform on the afterdeck. With a 20-round magazine, its cyclic rate of fire of 280 rounds per minute was hampered by frequent magazine changes, rendering its actual rate of fire closer to 120 rounds per minute. Its maximum range was about 4,900m horizontally or 3,700m vertically. In 1941 this design, which showed a tendency to jam, was superseded by the improved C/38 model. Both guns were mounted on a pedestal designated L/30. The combination of the gun and mount weighed approximately 420kg. This single mounting was manually operated and could be elevated to 85° and depressed to 11° below the horizontal. An LM 43 double mounting appeared in the later war period.

Beginning with boats in S 38 class, an additional 2cm C/38 gun was mounted in the bow where the gunner had a good field of fire and some protection. Early versions were mounted on a simple Scarff ring that was not well-suited for firing at aircraft. An improved design, the Drehkranzlafette 41, could deliver fire in a hemispherical arc, from 0° to 85° of elevation and with 360° of traverse. Its pantograph gunsight enabled the gunner to fire upwards at aircraft without crouching. Both versions of the bow gun could be stowed internally. For stowage, the barrel of the 2cm gun was detached, and the gun mount swung downwards on a hinge into the tub. A cover fit over the turret to protect it from rain and spray.

A small number of boats, including S 65, were field-equipped with the four-barreled 2cm Flakvierling around 1944. Each of the two firing pedals operated a pair of guns, each upper gun being coupled with the lower gun on the opposite side. The four C/38 guns could deliver a theoretical cyclic rate of fire of over 1,600 rounds per minute with all barrels firing. In practice, it was preferable to fire a single pair while the other pair was reloaded. The weapon had tremendous psychological impact, especially when firing tracer, but the seven-man gun crew was impractical and experience showed the 2cm round inadequate against MGBs.

Also beginning with the S 38 class and continuing into the S 100 class, numerous boats carried the 4cm Bofors gun on the afterdeck. The gun weighed approximately 521kg and had a rate of fire of 128 rounds per minute. Its maximum range was about 10,000 meters and it could be fired in either semi-automatic or automatic mode. While the 4cm Bofors was a reliable and effective weapon against air and sea targets, it lacked armor piercing shells, which Schnellboot command considered a requirement against MGBs.

The S 100 class sought to overcome this shortcoming with a fully automatic quick-firing 3.7cm Flak gun specially designed for shipboard use against attacking aircraft. Designated the 3.7cm Flak LM 42, it was shielded and could be fully operated by only three or four men. An experienced loader feeding five-round ammunition clips could maintain

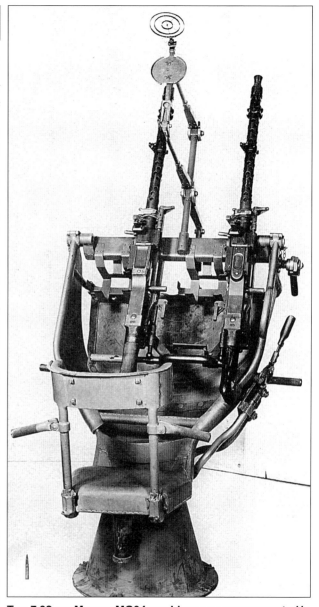

Two 7.92mm Mauser MG34 machine guns were mounted in the Zwillingsockel 36 (Twin Pedestal 36) turret, a common light anti-aircraft (AA) turret fitted to the S 38 classes. The MG34 had a muzzle velocity of 755m per second, a cyclic firing rate of 800 to 900 rounds per minute, and a maximum horizontal range of 4,570 meters. (U.S. Army Ordnance Museum, Aberdeen, Maryland)

The manually operated, single-mount, 2cm Rheinmetall MG C/38 cannon was the Kriegsmarine's standard light anti-aircraft gun. (U.S. Army Ordnance Museum)

The bow 2cm gunner was sometimes assisted by a loader. Ammunition stored below decks was passed through a hatch in the rear of the gun tub. (PK Langegger)

An S-Boot's 2cm MG/C30 crew takes aim during practice. For safety, a basket clipped to the weapon collects spent shell casings. One man uses binoculars to observe the target, while another instructs the gunner. One crewman loads an ammunition magazine, while another uses the hand wheel to raise the gun, which helps the gunner aim at a steep angle. (PK Steinmetz)

uninterrupted fire of 160-180 rounds per minute. The gun entered service in 1943 and had a range of about 6,600 meters at 45° and an anti-aircraft ceiling of 4,800 meters. Its arc of fire was -10° to 90° in the vertical plane and the mount had a 360° traverse. The mount, including the armored shield, weighed about 1,350kg. Less frequently, the 3.7cm Flak LM 43 U mount was used on later boats.

Other defensive armament included up to six depth charges and/or Schreckbombe. Used to discourage pursuit, Schreckbombe resembled depth charges but were floating mines with a time fuze. Large Nebelkanne NA 28 smoke generators facilitated evasion. Each was capable of delivering a thick cloud of gray smoke for up to half an hour and could be operated remotely from the wheelhouse. Smoke buoys of both German (Nebelboje-38) and French manufacture were stowed in ready positions on the aft deckhouses of wartime boats. They could be dropped overboard to establish a static smoke screen, mark a position, or misdirect the enemy by creating the appearance of a burning, disabled boat. Late in the war, many boats included an R Ag M 42 8.6cm rocket launcher.

The Kriegsmarine deployed S-Boote as minelayers as early as 1940 as a result of prewar experiments with S 14 - S 16. Various mine types were deployed, including the EMC, EMD, LMA, LMB, UMB, and the Soviet MO8 captured in Poland. More sophisticated magnetic/acoustic influence types included the TMA and TMB/S derived from the tube-launched mines developed for U-Boote. Removable rails were fixed to the deck edge at port and starboard for roll-off mines.

The compact, low-profile Drehkranz 41 was mainly fitted to S-Boote, but late-war Räumboote (R-Boote) also shared this gun, which was well suited for the small areas on the Schnellboot's bow and the R-Boot's wheelhouse roof. The Nachtsignalmast (night signal mast) seen here folded in its stowed position behind this R-Boot gunner, was another late-war feature common to both vessels. An IFF measure with four lights and adjustable color filters, the operator blinked one pair of lights as a challenge, the other to reply. It could also be used to flash coded light signals.

On the Drehkranz 41 mechanism, the handwheel on the gunner's right controlled elevation via a gear and ratchet. Counterbalance was provided by a tension spring. Traverse was accomplished by manually slewing the gun left or right on its ring. The mount was retracted by swinging it into the gun tub and removing the barrel. A cover protected the stowed mechanism and kept water out.

This photo affords a rare look at a late war S 100 class boat's unique bow gun arrangement. Characteristic of this type is the round inset area below deck level, on which five clips of ammunition were stowed with or without the cover in place. When the gun was readied for action, 10 additional clips were placed in the deck-level retainers. The clip retainer at the lower right of the photo is oriented fore and aft to provide clearance for the anchor chain. The shoulder brace is removed.

A Bootsmannsmaat (Boatswain's Mate Third Class) looks on as gunners practice aiming the bow 2cm gun, seen here elevated to nearly 90 degrees. The gunsight rotates in synch with the gun barrel on a separate axis, allowing the gunner to keep aircraft sighted without crouching. The petty officer wears a dark navy blue wool pea coat and black leather trousers favored for wet, cold, and windy conditions at sea. Helmets appear to be in factory-issue field green paint. (E. Krogh collection)

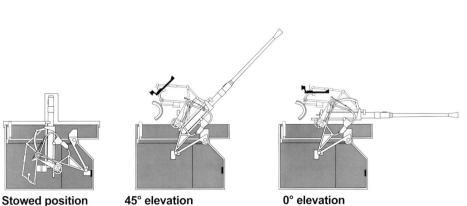

Stowed position
with cover   45° elevation   0° elevation

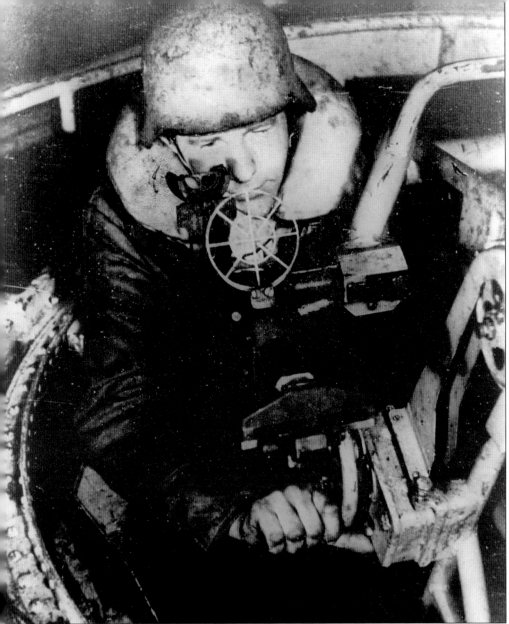

The original caption of this August 1944 PK photo states that this S-Boot bow gunner is engaged against the invasion fleet in the English Channel. As he operates the elevation handwheel, the position of the sight indicates the gun is at low elevation. The rear crosshairs have been modified by removing the top half. The gunner wears a black leather jacket with a small, yellow, crescent-shaped inflatable flotation device around his neck. These could be worn with or without a life vest and were ideal in cramped turrets. His helmet, originally issued in dark green, has been overpainted Schnellbootweiß, typical for helmets stowed externally. (PK Weinkauf)

Relaxing with a cigarette, S 91's bow gunner remains prepared for enemy aircraft with 11 clips of ready ammunition. It appears he has removed the top half of the cross hairs and favors operating his gun without the shoulder braces. The depression rail that ringed the turret prevented accidental firing into his own boat. The rail's starboard support post is offset to provide a clear path for the anchor chain. Ready ammunition was not stored on the starboard side for the same reason. Stowed on the deck behind him is the gun tub's circular cover with its vertical protrusion for the gun's receiver minus the barrel. Behind the cover and resting on the anchor is a rope fender. (E.J. Bakker collection)

Kriegsmarine 2cm Flak 38 auf MG C/38 Doppellafette LM 43

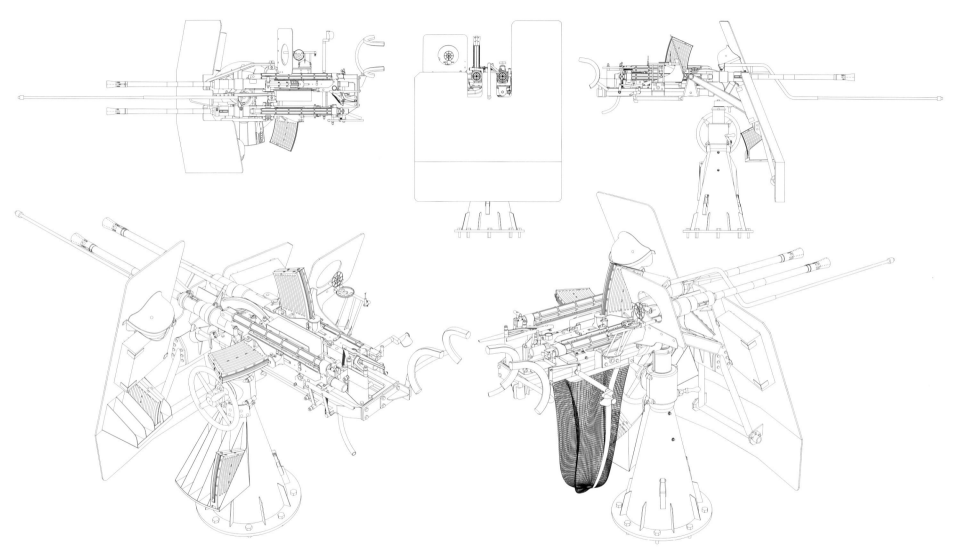

2cm Flak 38
Bore: 20mm
Length of Barrel: 1,300mm
Rate of Fire: 300 r.p.m. (approx)

Muzzle Velocity: 875m/s
Weight of projectile: 0.120kg
Elevation: -2° to +90°

Range: 4,800 meters at 45°
Ceiling: 3,700 meters at 90°
Drawings by Alin

Behind the 2cm Flak Doppellafette, Royal Navy officers examine the surrendered S 100 class boat *Lang* in 1945. *Lang* has late-war simplified torpedo cradles and enlarged ammunition lockers. (J. Lambert collection)

This snapshot from an S-Boot Geschützführer's album shows his seven-man crew posed at their 4cm Bofors gun. The number of men needed to operate this weapon was another drawback compared to the 3.7cm Flak. The platform sides are folded up.

A 4cm Bofors Flak 28 cannon is mounted on the aft deck of the armored S 38 class S-Boot S 91. This Swedish-designed weapon was built in occupied Norway under license for the Kriegsmarine. Clips of ready ammunition were stowed in lockers forward and aft of the gun. S 91's aft deck and superstructure were painted a dark gray. A pair of French-made smoke buoys are stowed on the port side, behind a canvas-covered reserve torpedo. S 91 has both a magnetic and a gyro compass in two binnacles. (E.J. Bakker Collection)

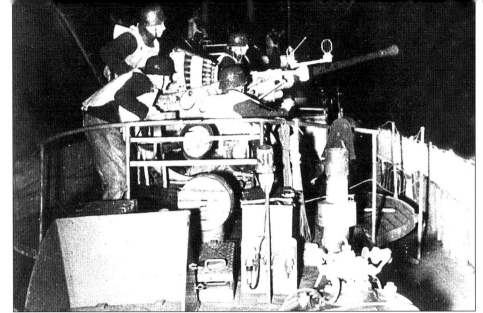

The crew of an unshielded 4cm Bofors prepare for night action on an S 38 class boat. S-Boote armed with this weapon took the rear position when retreating from an ambush to discourage pursuit. The Bofors gun's elevation range was -15° to +90° and its rate of fire was 128 rounds per minute. (PK Rolf Kröncke)

The Flak M 42 was specified as standard for the S 100 class in 1943. This weapon has a six-round ammunition clip loaded in its breech; the Flak M 42 normally used five-round clips at rate of 160-180 rounds per minute. The Flak M 42's effective anti-aircraft ceiling was 4,800m, while its range at 45° was 6,600m. (Royal Danish Navy)

Two sailors chip ice from the shielded 4cm cannon aboard S 91 during a winter cruise. A variety of Kriegsmarine designed and field-made splinter shields were fitted to Bofors guns. (E.J. Bakker collection)

Rheinmetall-Borsig specifically designed the 3.7cm Flak M 42 as a shipboard anti-aircraft weapon. It required a crew of only three or four men, ideal for use aboard smaller vessels. This Flak M 42 is fitted to an early C/36 mount. The wheels on the gun's right side control elevation, which ranges from -10° to +90°. The wheel on the left controls traverse. The gun is fired by depressing the foot pedal on the right. (Royal Danish Navy)

Kriegsmarine 3.7cm Flak M 42 Gun

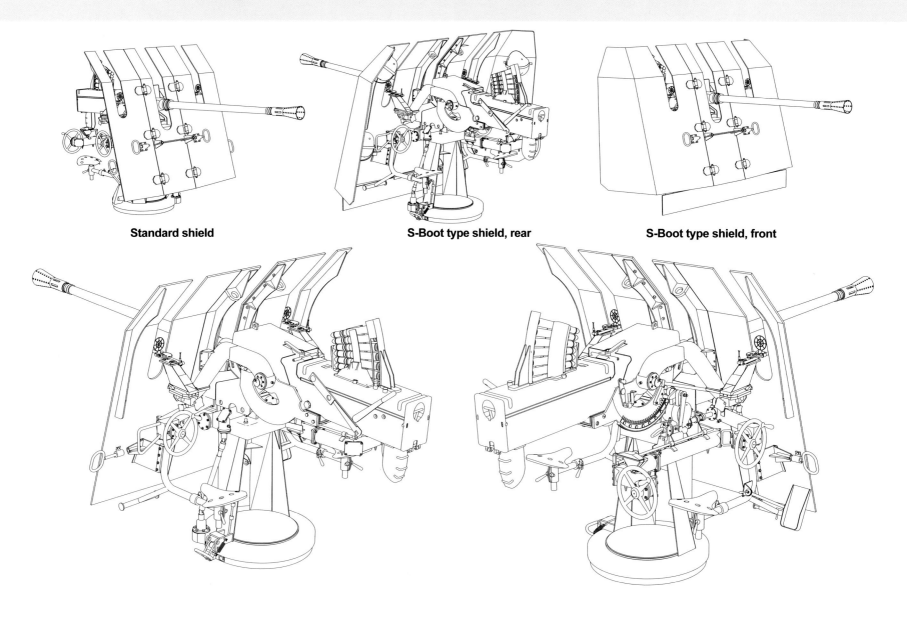

Standard shield   **S-Boot type shield, rear**   **S-Boot type shield, front**

Bore: 37mm
Weight of Gun: 300kg
Weight of Gun with Mount and Shield: 1,350kg
Length of Barrel: 2,560mm

Muzzle Velocity: 845m/s
Rate of Fire: 160 to 180 rounds per minute
Elevation: -10° to +90°
Traverse: 360°

Range: 6,600 meters at 45°
Ceiling: 4,900 meters at 90°
Barrel Life: 7,000 rounds
Manufacturer: Rheinmetall-Borsig

Three depth charges are mounted on the stern rack of a 1st Flotilla Schnellboot during a daylight anti-submarine sweep in the Black Sea. Each charge was released by manually disconnecting the cable that lashed it to the rack. This type was 44.5cm in diameter, 57cm wide, and weighed about about 190kg. The ends are yellow with red pistol covers, the case is dark gray. (PK Rolf Kröncke via PT Boats, Inc.)

Two units of the 2nd Flotilla prepare to depart Cherbourg harbor for a UMB anti-submarine mine laying sortie in 1943. S-Boote were effective as high-speed, clandestine minelayers. The rear boat, decorated with a red ace of hearts on its bulwarks, is Hans-Viktor Howaldt's S 89. (Klaus Feldt)

Sailors prepare an S 38 class boat for a mine laying mission in the Gulf of Finland. Crew attach mine rails to the decks while a Schreckbombe is hoisted to the flotilla tender. Although resembling a depth charge, this weapon was a floating mine used defensively to harass pursuing vessels. Its buoyancy chamber is oriented to the left in this photo. On the afterdeck, an overturned depth-charge rack awaits removal. Two baskets of bread lowered from the tender to the mid-deck will fortify the vessel's crew. (PK Hugo Bürger)

S 105's long-range radio operator works at his post below deck. The S Boot's radio room was located below the wheelhouse on the port side, with direct access to the captain's cabin. The Telefunken "Kurz Lang" 40/70 Watt Sende-Empfangs-Anlage Transmitter Receiver set and its associated electrical equipment is mounted on the forward bulkhead. The set consisted of an S 321 S 1/37 (S 4 a) transmitter and an E 382 bF (E 4 a) receiver. To the left, a civilian band receiver was also part of the radioman's equipment for morale and news. Below the radioman's desk and to his left is a small locker for code books and other secret documents. The varnished mahogany paneling was a typical interior feature throughout and reflected Lürssen's heritage of yacht building and craftsmanship. (PK Hugo Bürger)

A Rudergänger mans the wheel inside the enclosed wheelhouse, while a Funker mans the Lo 1 UK short-range Very High Frequency (VHF) radio set. The voice radio allowed rapid communication between flotilla vessels. A clock is mounted on the bulkhead over the helmsman's left shoulder, next to it is a pistol in its leather holster. The finely crafted wooden wheel and brass clock in this otherwise modern attack craft were tributes to naval tradition. (PK Rolf Kröncke)

Radio

Schnellboote most often operated at night in formations, making communication especially vital to navigation, formation keeping, target location, and attack coordination. A radioman stood by the helmsman as part of the bridge crew. He operated a short-range VHF voice transmitter receiver in the wheelhouse for rapid communications with other vessels in the flotilla. As in the Allied navies, boats were commonly identified by their captain's nicknames.

In the radio room forward and below the wheelhouse, a second radioman operated a short- and long-wave radio for ship-to-shore communication, general reception, and long-range communication. Mounted beneath a hinged panel in the center of the radio operator's desk in the radio room was an Enigma cipher machine for rapid encryption and decryption of coded messages. Below and to the left of the desk was a small safe where code books were kept under lock and key. The presence of the highly classified Enigma machine added to the boat's many capabilities and reflected the confidence and high value placed on individual Schnellboote by the Kriegsmarine's high command.

When conditions allowed, boats could communicate by lamps or semaphore flags. Prewar S-Boote had three pairs of red/white lamps in the mast for night signaling. Masts were removed during the war, but a short "night signal" mast was used on later boats.

Built by A.G. Neptun in Rostock, in 1940, Schnellbootsbegleitschiff *Adolf Lüderitz* weighs 3,600 tons and is 114 meters long. It was broken up 1964.

Built by A.G. Neptun in Rostock in 1939, Schnellbootsbegleitschiff *Tanga* weighs 2,620 tons and measures 96.2 meters in length. It was broken up 1967.

Built by A.G. Neptun in Rostock in 1940, Schnellbootsbegleitschiff *Carl Peters* weighs 3,600 tons and is 114 meters long. A mine sank it on 14 May 1945.

Built by Blohm + Voss in Hamburg in 1934, Schnellbootsbegleitschiff *Tsingtau* weighs 2,490 tons and measures 87.46 meters in length. It was broken up 1950.

The 8th Flotilla's S 38 class boat *Wulff* leads two other S-Boote out on a daylight patrol in 1943. The boat's name is painted on the side of the bridge. The Kommandant, Lt. Wulff Fanger, wears a captured French fleece jacket. A radio antenna mast is mounted on the aft starboard section of the bridge and a whimsical wooden parrot decorates the large loop-shaped Radio Direction Finding (RDF) antenna. When lowered, the canvas covers over the wheelhouse windows eliminated reflections and kept the glass clean. Immediately aft of the bridge is a canvas covered windbreak. (PK Tomann)

Navigation

Maneuvering a Schnellboot in combat required precision navigation and steering under the most trying of conditions. The S-Boot's few navigational tools were laid out in a simple and logical manner. The navigator plotted the course on a small table in the rear of the wheelhouse. Several compasses were carried on board; a central compass was mounted amidships in a binnacle. The captain, navigator, and helmsman had smaller compasses mounted in their respective positions. Reserve compasses were mounted in various positions around the boat. Many boats were equipped with an echo sounder to assist in navigating shallow waters.

Radio direction finding (RDF) equipment was standard. Although not always mounted, its distinctive loop antenna fitted into a socket at the rear of the wheelhouse. The RDF was used to pinpoint the boat's precise position by triangulating radio transmissions from known positions ashore. A skilled operator could use it to locate the position from which an enemy ship was transmitting.

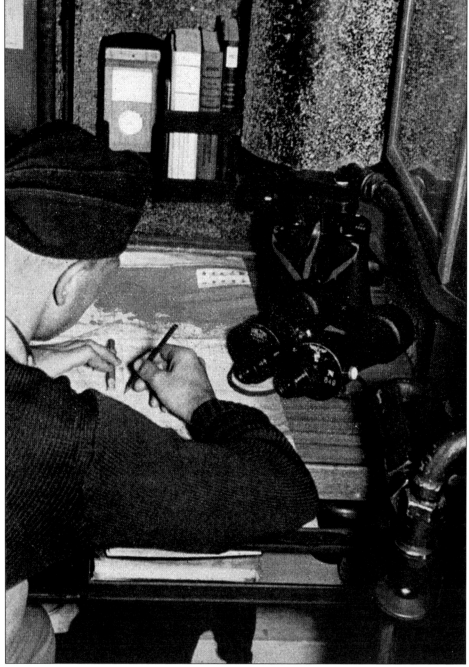

The navigator plots the S-Boot's course at his desk in the wheelhouse. The Kommandant will consult the navigator and his charts through a shuttered window connecting this small cabin and the bridge. The interior bulkheads were painted with a non-reflective, cork-textured black paint. It appears that the captain and his first officer have left their Zeiss 7x50 binoculars on the navigator's table for safekeeping. (PK Hugo Bürger)

Radar and Detection

Schnellboote relied chiefly on constant radio contact with shore-based radar installations and visual/radio monitoring stations for long-distance location of, and vectors to, enemy ships. Shore-based radar was effective to within 18km of the English coast in good weather, and developed to great efficiency closer to the occupied coast. German hydrophones (a sensitive directional microphone array mounted outside the hull, below the waterline) were also effective. These devices were able to locate a PT boat traveling at 30 knots from a range of 18km. Functional even while underway, they emitted no tell-tale signals to the enemy and were thus preferred to radar, although performance was degraded as the speed of the detecting vessel increased.

After an initial lead, Germany began to lag seriously behind the Allies in the development and use of ship-mounted naval radar. Nevertheless, the Kriegsmarine sought to equip some S-Boote with appropriately small radar antenna. The earliest application was the FuMo 71 "Lichtenstein B/C," a fixed radar array measuring about 1.3m x 1.6m that could scan a 35-degree arc ahead of the boat. Its range was limited – only about two to six kilometers – but it was extremely accurate for ranging and navigationally useful in

The 4th Flotilla's S 202 *Jochen* is moored in the Hellinggat Canal at Maassluis, Netherlands, in the winter of 1944-1945. On the mast are FuMB 24 (upper) and FuMB 32 (lower) directional radar sensors. The operator directly aft of the bridge cockpit rotated this mast a full 360° to detect enemy radar emissions. A number 8 pennant flies from the radio antenna on the starboard side of the Kalotte, indicating the crew is on watch duty. In the background, De Grote Kerk's bell tower pinpoints the location.

darkness and fog. It was adapted from the Luftwaffe's obsolete FuG202 and went into limited service on Schnellboote in late 1943. Experiments were made with this antenna mounted to a rotatable mast. This configuration, designated FuMO 72, further enlarged the radar signature of the S-Boot itself, earning it the derisive name "artillery shell collection basket." Only three sets were field tested before it was deemed unsatisfactory.

In March 1944, the FuMo 62 "Hohentwiel S," developed for picket ships, was tested for Schnellboot use. It was also based on a Luftwaffe set, the FuG 200 Hohentwiel ASV (anti-surface vessel) radar. It had a greater range – about 10km – and more accuracy than the FuMo 71, however, the 1.2m x 1.2m rotating antenna caused a similar unacceptable increase in radar signature. At least two boats, S 122 and S 127, served as the testbeds for the FuMo 81 "Berlin S" type radar in 1944. The Berlin radar was an outgrowth of the Luftwaffe's "Rotterdam" apparatus. It was an efficient microwave search radar that operated on a 9cm wavelength with a peak power of 18kW-20kW and an effective range of about 30km. The rotating antenna consisted of four end-firing plastic rods housed under a Plexiglas dome mounted on a bipod mast behind the bridge – an arrangement that was a precursor to the modern naval "radome."

None of the sets evaluated met with as great a success as their counterparts on British and American boats. Recognizing the disparity between the high-quality Allied radar and the less than satisfactory German sets, the ever resourceful German engineers developed a number of effective radar counter measures, including passive radar detection and ranging. Radar detection gear gave early warning of enemy forces based on their radar emissions while still beyond the useful range of the enemy's own radar. The apparatus effectively enabled the S-Boot to detect and generally locate the enemy's presence without being located itself.

The FuMB Ant 3 antenna, codenamed "Bali 1," was a commonly used passive radar detection sensor. The "Bali 1" antenna was part of the FuMB 29 "Bali-Anlage" radar surveillance system. It could be used with a FuMB 4 "Samos" reciever (90-470 MHz), a FuMB 9 frequency indicator (146-264 MHz), or a FuMB 10 "Borkum" signal detector (100-400 MHz). The signals were fed through a booster to an FuMZ 1 oscilloscope, where they would be viewed and interpreted by the operator.

A similar detector, FuMB 32 "Flores" was developed specifically for the S-Boot (100-300 MHz) and began service in 1944. It was capable of direction finding, and was mounted on a light rotating mast. It was approximately 25cm in diameter and also used the "Samos" receiver. The FuMB 24 "Cuba 1a," also known as "Fliege," provided relatively accurate long-range detection, particularly in the 9cm wavelength, and its compact antenna was ideal for Schnellboot use. A "Flores" and a "Fliege" antenna were usually fitted to the same mast, which rotated via a handwheel in the operator's cabin directly behind the bridge.

The "Naxos" detectors FuMB23 and FuMB28 began service on Schnellboote in mid 1944 and utilised a futuristic rotating detector unit housed under a Plexiglas radome referred to as antenna type ZA 290M. They provided accurate long-range directional location of enemy radar signals from air or sea, particularly in the 9cm wavelength.

Other detection units included the FuMB 26 "Tunis" antenna, used on several of the S 151 and S 30 class boats in the Mediterranean. Numerous other units were in the testing stages towards the end of the war. These included the 2-20cm wavelength detection multi-antenna "Libyen," housed in a rectangular box resembling a traffic light, as well as the portable FuMB 33 "Lilliput" detection gear for the 9cm range, intended for use on the LS boats and other small craft.

The Germans further exploited the weakness of enemy radar by deploying radar decoy buoys, as used on U-Boote. The buoys mimicked the radar signature of a Schnellboot to confuse the enemy. Other experimentation attempted to find materials that would conceal the boats from enemy radar by absorbing or scattering radio signals. A reflection dimming rubberized coating known as "Tarnmatte" was developed and used on U-Boote. Although tests to camouflage S-Boote using measures similar to "Tarnmatte" were partially successful at certain wavelengths, apparently the system did not develop to operational use.

Experiments with passive infra-red night vision equipment showed great promise, but by the end of the war even the most advanced versions still required a fairly steady platform and clear weather conditions, rendering them ineffective in fog or on moderate seas. Passive infra-red night-vision devices were used with success on heavier ships and by land-based observation points.

Three antenna are fixed to the mast on the rear of this S 100 class boat's wheelhouse. A cylindrical FuMB 25 "Mucke" sensor tops a FuMB 32 "Flores" in the middle, and a FuMB 24 "Fliege" is at the bottom. These provided directional, long range radar detection to warn of enemy presence. A night signal mast is at right.

Radar and Radio Antenna

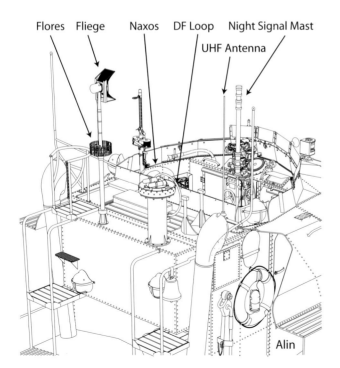

Flores   Fliege   Naxos   DF Loop   Night Signal Mast
UHF Antenna
Alin

The FuMB 23 and similar FuMB28 "Naxos" detectors both used ZA 290M antennas, which were enclosed within a clear radome. This long-range radar detector entered S-Boot service in mid-1944. (U.S. Naval Technical Mission / U.S. Naval Historical Center)

Several S 151 and S 30 boats deployed in the Mediterranean were equipped with the FuMB 26 "Tunis" radar detector. This device was a combination of FuMB 25 "Mucke" and FuMB 24 "Fliege" antenna. (U.S. Naval Technical Mission / U.S. Naval Historical Center)

Camouflage, Colors, and Insignia

The first boats were painted in the German Navy's traditional Hellgrau 50 light gray. Methodical pre-war experimentation confirmed what seamen had noticed for centuries: that at sea after dark, small, light-colored vessels were more difficult to see than darker-colored ones. Although this seems counter-intuitive, very light shades blend with the horizon line between sea and sky. Since Schnellboot tactics called primarily for operations under the cover of darkness, starting in 1937, vertical surfaces were factory painted a very pale gray appropriately referred to as "Schnellbootweiß."

Below the waterline, boats were painted Schiffsbodenfarbe Grau 23a or 23b antifouling gray, or Schiffsbodenfarbe Rot 22a or 22b anti-fouling red. Horizontal surfaces varied from very dark to light gray. Olive green was also used on decks, although infrequently. Deck treatments served as camouflage from air observation, hid scuff marks from the crew's boots, and provided some traction. Maintenance and cleanliness were emphasized; the hardworked S-Boote were kept remarkably clean.

Disruptive camouflage patterns on the vertical surfaces were mainly confined to the Scandinavian theater of operations, where short summer nights, proximity to shore, and the lack of bunkers negated the camouflage value of Schnellbootweiß. Variations on an oblong splotch pattern (probably locally mixed grays and Hellbraun 36.1 light brown) were most common, although a gray splinter scheme, and a mottled brown scheme were also used in Norwegian waters. Boats involved in Operation Weserübung, the April 1940 invasion of Norway, were still in the standard Schnellbootweiß scheme.

On the Channel Front, disruptive camouflage patterns were few and limited to the early war period. At least one S 30 class boat at Ostende is seen with a rough crosshatch pattern of deck gray applied over the upper vertical surfaces. In French ports, there were some attempts to reduce visibility from the air by breaking up the gray horizontal surfaces with irregular patches of Schnellbootweiß. A pink-tinted variation of Schnellbootweiß used in the English Channel was considered effective.

Following pre- and early-war protocols for German vessels training in the Baltic and North Sea, colored panels were sometimes painted on the afterdecks for air recognition. Sections of the decks of S-Boote taking part in Operation Cerberus were painted bright yellow: from the stern to the aft deckhouse, and from the bow to the wheelhouse. Boats serving in the Black Sea displayed red/white air recognition stripes at the bow, following the Italian practice. A supplemental Black Sea air recognition measure specified a bright yellow St. Andrew's Cross to be painted on a forward horizontal surface; in coordination with the Luftwaffe, the color was to be changed periodically.

In addition to painted recognition and camouflage measures, Schnellboote carried an assortment of national flags, Allied and neutral, that could be flown in order to confuse coastwatchers and enemy ships. These foreign flags were official Kriegsmarine issue.

Beginning in late 1935 or early 1936, a relief-cast bronze-colored eagle was applied to the bulwarks on either side of the wheelhouse. These, along with hull numbers, were removed as a wartime security measure in late 1939. In 1945, under orders from the Allies, hull numbers were again painted on the bows for inventory purposes.

By decree of Großadmiral Erich Raeder on 30 May 1941, a distinctive badge was designed for Schnellboot personnel. It was awarded to crew who participated in 12 operational missions or were wounded through enemy action. Official issue commenced in October 1941. Apparently the first badge, which depicted an S 30 class boat, was not well-received and a second pattern, depicting an S 38 class boat, was authorized in January of 1943. Prior to October 1941, qualifying S-Boot crewmen wore the destroyer badge. The eight S-Boot captains who earned Oak Leaves to the Knight's Cross were each awarded the Schnellboot badge with diamonds.

An S 38 class S-Boot cruises at high speed in the Baltic Sea. This vessel was camouflaged for daytime operations against Soviet shipping. The camouflage consisted of dark blue and blue gray waves on the Schnellbootweiß base color. (PK Schwarz via P. Rezmann)

Although camouflage was relatively uncommon, a pattern of long splotches is the most frequently encountered in photographs, as in this dramatic view of an S 38 type on patrol in the Baltic. (PK Schwarz)

S 113 cruises in Norwegian waters off Svolvær in 1942. This 6th S-Bootsflottille vessel is painted in hard-edged splotches of browns and grays over the Schnellbootweiß finish. The camouflage better matched the snow-covered fjord landscape than did solid pale gray. (E.J. Bakker collection)

Another 6th Flotilla S 38 class boat departs Svolvær harbor during its short 1942 deployment to Norway. Its crew painted the brown and gray splotches in a pattern different from that on its sister boat. The oblong splotch pattern seems to have its origins in a similar, earlier pattern used on Finnish torpedo boats. (E.J. Bakker collection)

The 1st Flotilla's S 102 cruises astern of another S-Boot in the Black Sea. The bow is painted in diagonal red and Schnellbootweiß stripes as an air recognition measure. As a supplemental measure for German vessels, a bright yellow cross is painted over the gun tub cover. The rest of the deck is either gray or possibly an olive green, which was infrequently applied to boats in coastal waters. This early S 38 class boat is retrofitted with the first pattern 2cm bow gun. (PK Rolf Kröncke)

This Lürssen S 2 class export variant was built for Bulgaria but requisitioned by the Kriegsmarine and commissioned as S 1 (II) in September 1939. It was nicknamed *Mäxchen*. In March 1941 it was delivered to Bulgaria and commissioned as F (Torpedo Boat) 3. Captured by the Soviets in September 1944, it was taken into the Black Sea Fleet as TK (Torpedo Boat) 960. Returned to Bulgaria in July 1945, it served as a minesweeper until 1953, then Admiral's Launch 622 from 1956 until it was scrapped in 1975.

BULGARIAN NAVY

Jack

Ensign
(1878-1944)

Flotilla Chief

BADAJOZ

Wheelhouse roof

In 1938 Germany sold five decommissioned S-Boote – S 1 to S 5 – to the Spanish Nationalist Navy. Though refurbished by Lürssen, these were obsolete experimental boats of doubtful naval value. Nevertheless they were the first of a fleet of 17 boats which were to serve Spain into the 1970s. S 1 commissioned as *Badajoz,* then renamed LT (Torpedo Boat) 13, and decommissioned in 1940.

An unidentified unit of the 8th Flotilla stationed in the Semske-Fjord in Northern Norway in 1942 displays a splinter camouflage scheme of dark gray, or blue gray, over Schnellbootweiß. This form of camouflage is seldom seen in photographs and was probably limited to boats deployed to Norwegian waters.

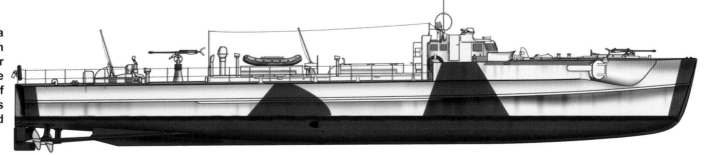

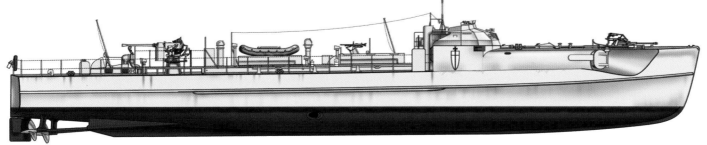

Under the command of Oberbootsmannsmaat Bernhard Theenhausen, the 9th Flotilla's S 147 was sunk by the French destroyer *La Combattante* in the English Channel on 26 April 1944. Royal Navy prisoner interrogation report C.B. 040501 records the boat's vertical surfaces were "white tinged with pink."

KM Nr.	KM Color Designation	Description	FS 595B Approximation	
22 a	Schiffsbodenfarbe I Rot	Anti Fouling I Red	20152	
23 b	Schiffsbodenfarbe III Grau	Anti Fouling III Gray	36081	
32.2	Blaugrau Mittel	Medium Blue Gray	25190	
36.1	Tarnfarbe Hellbraun	Camouflage Light Brown	33522	
50	Hellgrau	Prewar Light Gray	36375	
53	Trittfeste Außendecksfarbe Grau	Scuff / Slip Resistant Exterior Dark Gray	26187	
60	Schnellbootweiß / Deckfarbe Weiß	Schnellboot White / Very Light Gray	27875	
90	Schlauchbootfarbe Taubengrau	Rubberized Canvas Pigeon Gray	24158	

1921 - 1933   1933 - 1935   1935 - 1945

(Right) S 7 was the lead boat in its class of seven Schnellboote. When it began service in 1934, it was painted in the traditional Kriegsmarine Hellgrau 50 scheme with white bow numbers. In late 1935 or early 1936 the bulwarks were decorated with a bronze eagle, and in 1937 it was painted in Schnellbootweiß 60 with black bow numbers. Decks were medium to dark gray and the hull below the waterline was Anti fouling Grau 23 b.

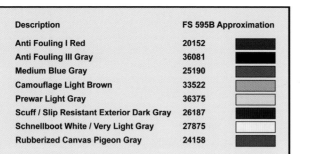

(Right) This early S 38 class vessel was assigned to the 2nd S-Bootsflottille in Finland in 1941. Splotches painted over the Schnellbootweiß 60 base finish were in two shades of gray, probably locally mixed, and Hellbraun 36.1. The personal insignia depicting an osprey carrying a torpedo (below) was painted in black and shades of gray on a white field.

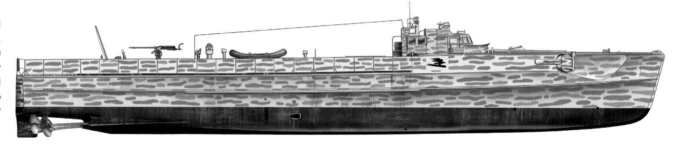

(Right) Boats deployed to southern theaters of the Black Sea and Mediterranean were occasionally painted with Red and Schnellbootweiß diagonal stripes on the bow. This marking was adopted from Italian practice and reduced the risk of "friendly fire" from Axis aircraft. The width and number of stripes varied.

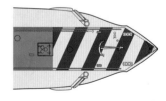

(Left) Another early S 38 class Schnellboot was assigned to daylight operations against Soviet shipping in the Eastern Baltic in 1941. It was camouflaged in Mittelblaugrau 32.2 and gray over Schnnellbootweiß 60. The rigid life raft is covered in rubberized pigeon gray canvas.

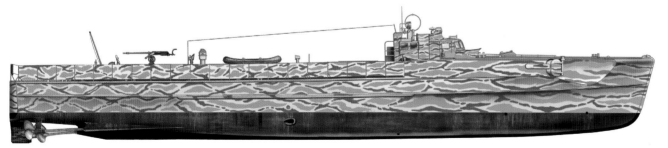

72

This refit S 38 class vessel operated with the 2nd S-Bootsflottille in the English Channel in 1942. A 40mm Bofors cannon is mounted on the after deck for use against aircraft and surface vessels. Schiffsbodenfarbe I red anti-fouling paint coated the boat's below-waterline surfaces and replaced the earlier Schiffsbodenfarbe III black-gray anti-fouling paint. Two "Ace of Hearts" cards were painted on the bridge wind deflector, flanking a gold hose shoe talisman.

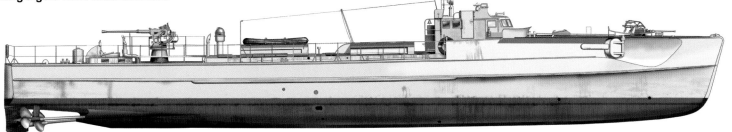

This Armored S 38 class boat named *Walter* was assigned to the 8th S-Bootsflottille for operations in the North Sea and English Channel in 1943-1944. Horizontal surfaces, as well as deckhouses and ventilators aft of the armored bridge, are painted a scuff resistant dark gray.

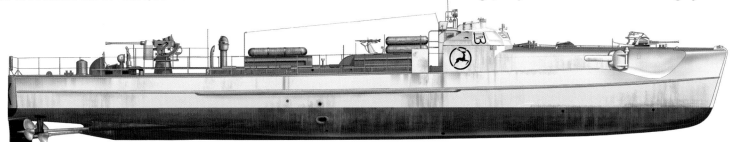

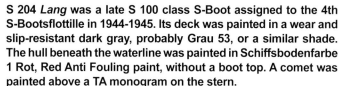

4th Flotilla Insignia

S 204 *Lang* was a late S 100 class S-Boot assigned to the 4th S-Bootsflottille in 1944-1945. Its deck was painted in a wear and slip-resistant dark gray, probably Grau 53, or a similar shade. The hull beneath the waterline was painted in Schiffsbodenfarbe 1 Rot, Red Anti Fouling paint, without a boot top. A comet was painted above a TA monogram on the stern.

Lang

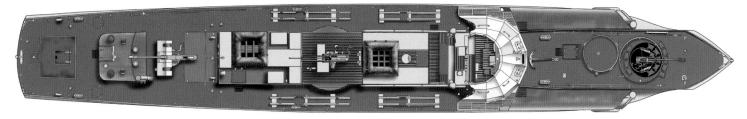

The first (left) and second (right) pattern Schnellboot war merit badges were worn on the lower left breast of the uniform. The first, instituted May 1940, depicts an S 30 type. Uniquely among German badges, the design was superceded in January 1943, to show a sleeker, more aggressive S 38 type Schnellboot.

A training exercise in home waters of the Baltic is an opportunity for daylight formation practice as well as some rare color photography. The paint scheme is Schnellbootweiß, with dark gray decks and deckhouses up to the Kalotte. The 2cm Zwilling gun shield in the foreground is decorated with a green four-leaf clover.

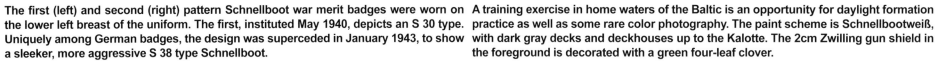

An S 38 class boat at high speed shows off its classic Schnellboot lines and color scheme. Its nearly white sides contrast with the dark red anti fouling paint, and its near black anti-slip painted decks.

Weathering and rust on the depth charges indicate that no enemy submarines have been spotted recently. The life ring is painted red with white stripes; solid red is also typical. A Rettungsbojenlicht flare in its red cannister is attached to the ring with rope.

A Maat (Petty Officer) attaches two kill pennants to his S-Boot's radio antenna mast. Each pennant is marked with the approximate tonnage of the enemy vessel sunk. These banners were displayed when the boat returned to port after a successful sortie. He wears a pneumatic life vest as much for safety as a bit of extra warmth. (PK Rolf Kröncke)

Tactics and Deployment

"It is incomparably more effective to sink a whole cargo than to have to fight the unloaded personnel and material separately on land at a later date," – thus summarized Hitler the underlying strategy of Schnellboot operations. Early in the war, Schnellboot captains pressed home many daring close-quarters attacks on Allied merchant ships and convoys. Luftwaffe reconnaissance and air support enabled them to travel to and from distant ambush areas during daylight hours. However the tactics employed against the Western Allies grew more conservative in the light of the Allies' growing defences and of the Schnellboote flotillas' thinning ranks. A June 1944 U.S. Navy intelligence report summarized Schnellboot operations as follows:

"E-Boats favor night conditions of mist and calm sea and luminous conditions such as a half moon. They leave their bases in packs and on reaching the convoy lanes, split into flotillas of six. Boats with the 40mm take stern positions in formation. They move in column formation and are generally given accurate radar information from shore. Using hydrophones and elementary radar, they move slowly and quietly up for attack (they may lay quiet moored to a Channel buoy) and after firing their torpedoes use evasive tactics similar to PTs. The flotilla leaders decide the tactics, and their policy up to the present has been to avoid combat. These boats attack British small craft only if the prey is crippled or vastly inferior in fire power . . . .

"E-Boats are high speed torpedo boats; neither hull nor armament are capable of resisting the slower British boats. Committed to a policy of conservation of their numbers, they decline gunnery duels. They shadow stragglers or damaged boats, make quick runs and break away, and even conclusive superiority recently has failed to lure them into point blank range. Their marksmanship is mediocre unless given a point of fire by long bursts of tracers. They fire high and often fail to close to effective range before firing.

"British craft cannot catch them and rarely attempt a running fight with them. When encountered, E-Boats usually run in formation on the flotilla leader, turning away by a sharp movement to right or left from column. When circumstances force them to scatter, they apparently have a prearranged rendezvous at certain bearing and distance from any scramble."

Conclusion

For Germany, the naval war was mainly a war of U-Boote and coastal craft in which the Schnellboot played a significant, if not outsized, role. Unlike the beleaguered capital units of the Kriegsmarine's surface fleet, throughout the war the Schnellboote saw constant action against increasing Allied strength, a widening radar technology gap, and shrinking industrial capacity on the home front. By the end of the war, the Schnellboot was the Kriegsmarine's last remaining surface unit still capable of effective offensive action against Allied shipping. But in the war's final days, it served a humanitarian mission: assisting in the mass seaborne evacuation of German civilians and soldiers from the Baltic States.

Their accomplishments were impressive. In the English Channel, Baltic Sea, Black

S 26, operating off Finland in 1941, lays down a smoke screen from its deck-mounted smoke generators. This smoke shielded the boat from the eyes of enemy vessels, particularly when retiring from an engagement. The Reichskriegsflagge flies smartly from the flagstaff amidships. The wave camouflage pattern is painted on the inboard side of the canvas dodgers. (PK Schwarz)

In a scene familiar to torpedo boat crews of all navies, the bridge crew of this S 38 class boat keeps a sharp watch for potential targets. (PT Boats, Inc. collection)

Starting a patrol, one S-Boot cruises astern of another beneath a setting sun. They will soon be cloaked in darkness, giving them a tactical advantage. (PK Rolf Kröncke)

Sea, North Sea, Mediterranean Sea and Barents Sea, Schnellboote sank 156 cargo ships totaling 405,000 tons, and 15 tankers totaling 60,000 tons. They also sank a passenger liner, a hospital ship, 10 destroyers, 7 destroyer escorts, 3 submarines, 6 landing ships, 6 landing craft, 15 minesweepers, 8 PT boats, 3 MGBs, 21 patrol boats, 45 trawlers, 10 tug boats, and numerous other small vessels. Mines laid by Schnellboote sank at least an additional 37 merchant ships totaling 148,535 tons, a destroyer, two minesweepers, and four landing ships. The final tally was over half a million tons of Allied shipping sent to the bottom and many vessels damaged. Yet this was little more than a nuisance relative to the sheer mass of Allied production.

The intensity of combat is indicated by the 23 Knight's Cross recipients produced by the Schnellboot service, eight of whom were further distinguished with the oak leaves, and by the 112 German Cross in Gold recipients. It is likewise indicated by the 767 Schnellboot crewmen killed in action, 620 wounded and 322 taken prisoner.

The Schnellboot was an investment in the concept that quality and skill will outclass mass production on the battlefield. The concept, though tactically correct, did not account for the strategic strain on Germany's manufacturing and fighting capabilities over the course of a lengthy two-front war. The Schnellboot was probably the most capable and effective torpedo boat of WWII; its design was ingenious, its crews were well led and fought gallantly, but in the final analysis, Allied demographics and mass production proved insurmountable.

Dry-docked boats allotted to Denmark by the Office of Military Government of the United States (OMGUS) await overhaul and recommissioning in the Royal Danish Navy in August of 1947. Hull numbers – strictly banned by wartime security – reappeared as a post-war Allied inventory measure. S 97, docked at lower right, was the second longest surviving Schnellboot, albeit in derelict condition. It was scrapped in 2004 after a failed salvage effort. (L. Alring / Royal Danish Navy)

S-Boote await Allied orders in Den Helder, the Netherlands, immediately after the German capitulation in 1945. Among these boats are elements of the 5th and 6th S-Bootsflottillen. The cruciform object in the lower center is the field-modified depression rail striker of a twin 2cm Flak. The boat at lower left is armed with a 3.7cm LM 43 U. (E.J. Bakker collection)

The flag lowering ceremony in Geltinger Bay on 10 May 1945 commemorated the final moments of the Kriegsmarine's Schnellboot fleet. Here, from the quarterdeck of the Flotilla tender *Hermann von Wissmann,* Kommodore Rudolf Petersen, Führer der Schnellboote, addresses the paraded crews of the still combat ready 10th Flotilla and the 3rd Training Flotilla. Even in defeat, the resolute spirit and discipline of these fighting men is evident in their orderly formation. The boat with the large G marking is the 10th Flotilla's S 305 *Günther.*

Restoration

Numerous boats survived the war and were allotted to the victor nations as war prizes. Beginning in 1947, a total of 18 served in the Danish Navy until the last (ex-S 68) decommissioned in 1965. As late as 1975 the S 2 export type, ex-Kriegsmarine S 1 (II), was actively serving the Bulgarian Navy as Admiral's Launch 622.

Today, the entire Schnellboot fleet is sunken or scrapped, with but a single exception: S 130. Built by Schlichting and commissioned on 21 October 1943, S 130 served under her Kommandant, Kptlt. Günter Rabe, in the 9th S-Boot Flotilla in the English Channel. S 130 took part in the battle of Slapton Sands, in which several U.S. LSTs (landing ship, tank) participating in mock invasion exercises were attacked. The engagement took the lives of 197 American seamen and 441 soldiers, more than three times the casualties on Utah Beach. In 1945, S 130 was taken as a British war prize and subsequently put to use in covert operations in the Baltic.

Incredibly, this boat survived close combat, decay, and perhaps most threatening of all, decades of financial and political pressures that sent many other historic naval vessels to the scrappers. S 130 earned its keep in postwar years by serving various purposes and masters, from spy ferry for the British intelligence service MI6, to underwater explosives training boat for the West German Bundesmarine, under the pennant number

The Kriegsmarine's former S 206 and S 127 are recommissioned as T-55 (left) and T-56, respectively, of the Royal Danish Navy in 1947. They appear well-maintained and unchanged from their original configuration. The Danes renamed T-55 as *Högen* (P555) and T-56 as *Isfuglen* (P556) in 1951. (L. Alring/Royal Danish Navy)

Antennas bristle on the deck of the Danish vessel *Hejrin,* formerly S 117, in 1960. The Danes refitted this S 38 class boat several times after acquiring it from Norway in 1951. This boat mounts a drum-fed 2cm Luftwaffe MGFF cannon in the bow. Welds on the Kalotte joined armor plates, while light sheet metal was bonded with rivets. (L. Alring/ Royal Danish Navy)

The Danish boat T-52 (ex-S 107) cruises off the Danish coast. This vessel mounts a pair of 2cm Flak Zwilling, an unusual arrangement for an S-Boot. The Danes widened the depression rail striker bars by a safe margin. Vertical surfaces are two shades of gray, with black bow numbers. T-52 was renamed *Gribben* (P552) in 1951 and stricken nine years later. (L. Alring/Royal Danish Navy)

Hejrin (P566) has been thoroughly modernized with North Atlantic Treaty Organization (NATO) standard 53.3cm torpedo tubes, electronics, and a coat of dark green paint. Nevertheless, this fine portrait evokes its proud heritage as the Kriegsmarine's S 117. The pennant number on the side of the hull below the Kalotte was standard for NATO vessels. She is armed with one 2cm cannon in the bow and a 4cm cannon on the aft deck. *Hejrin* and *Viben* (P568, formerly S 68 and T-62) were decommissioned in 1965 – the last of the ex-Kriegsmarine S-Boote to serve in the Royal Danish Navy. (L. Alring/Royal Danish Navy)

Under its first commander, Oberleutnant zur See Günter Rabe, S 130 serves in the 9th Flotilla.

UW 10, and finally, EF 3. Each new role altered its appearance somewhat so that upon decommissioning in 1991 and subsequent use as a houseboat, the vessel was a shadow of its original design. Only the hull retained the unmistakable sleek lines of a Schnellboot.

In 2003, S 130 was privately purchased from its German owners for restoration in the UK in cooperation with the British Military Powerboat Trust in Southampton. After a risky but successful cross-Channel tow and some initial conservation work, the financial and logistical burdens of a full restoration proved too great and work ceased, leaving the boat to an uncertain future.

While at Southampton, S 130 attracted the attention of Kevin Wheatcroft, well known for his collection of WWII German armor, meticulous restoration work, and commitment to historical accuracy. Wheatcroft purchased the vessel and began restoring it to original wartime configuration. Completing this massive project will require millions of dollars and many thousands of man hours over the course of several years.

To ensure maximum originality and accuracy, a marine salvage company was contracted to recover replacement parts – like the armored wheelhouse seen on this page – from S-Boot wrecks off the Danish coast. These boats were scuttled by the Kriegsmarine in 1945 to keep them out of British hands, ironically creating a parts cache for a British restoration 60 years later. Many other salvaged parts await restoration and final fitting out.

Upon completion, S 130, which played a significant part in the battle for control over the English Channel, will be a testament to naval engineering and craftsmanship, and a reminder of the bravery of the men who went to war on boats like these.

After restoration, this salvaged wheelhouse will replace S 130's missing wheelhouse. (B. Balkwill)

S 130 moves into its temporary enclosure in March 2008. Despite its many alterations, the hull still shows the sleek, powerful lines of a Schnellboot. (B. Balkwill)